EXEC

ASSISTANT

MASTERY

How to Make the Biggest Impact to Your

Manager in 90 days

A 43 Step Process for Corporate

Executive Assistants

MARIA FULLER

Executive Assistant Mastery
Copyright © 2023 Maria Fuller

ISBN 978-0-9933837-1-7

About the Author

Maria Fuller is an accomplished UK executive assistant with 30 years of experience in the business administration sector. She is known for her dedication to excellence, and her commitment to helping executives achieve their goals. Maria is passionate about sharing her knowledge and expertise with others in the profession. This is her second book, it is based upon her experience as a C-suite assistant, and her desire to empower executive assistants to reach their full potential.

Introduction

Thank you for purchasing Executive Assistant Mastery. I hope you find it a super useful resource, on your game changing journey to EA mastery. This is my second book. My first book 'How to be a PA' was published in 2016 and reached the no. 1 bestseller position in its category on Amazon UK, Germany, and France.

If you aren't familiar with it, please check it out on Amazon. It covers everything a personal assistant, executive assistant, and administrative professional, needs to know to get started in the role.

You might be asking yourself, what makes 'Maria Fuller' an EA authority, and a credible author? Well, I've worked full-time, as an executive assistant in the UK, for 2 decades. I have 10 years' experience directly at CEO level, and an additional 10 years supporting C-level executives. Before that, I worked as a PA / administrative professional, so I've racked up a total of 30 years' service, in the business support sector.

I worked my way up from ground-level as a secretary, then specialised as a legal secretary, and then moved into personal assistant roles. Supporting teams, managers, and then regional directors. Today, I work at the highest level, as EA to the CEO.

My last 'contract' role was supporting the CEO of a private equity investment platform, called Titanbay. My last 'permanent' role was supporting the CEO of Teleperformance UK. That CEO was responsible for 10,000 employees, across 27 different sites. I've also supported a CEO of a biotech start-up with 100 employees during a series C funding round, where we secured $125M of investment.

Introduction

Throughout my career, I've held various EA positions based in London, and Bristol, and now I work remotely from my beautiful coastal location in sunny Devon, in the southwest of the UK.

I'm an expert at business travel management, having arranged in excess of 5,000 trips, globally and domestically. Yes, 5,000! But I don't just book flights and drop them into the calendar, I provide what I call a 'door to door' travel and logistics service.

I plan every step of my CEO's trip; from the moment he leaves his home address to the moment he arrives at his destination. I block out time for ground transfers, airport check-ins, flight times, hotel check-ins and check-outs, and I ensure all corresponding booking confirmations are embedded into the calendar, for my CEO to access with ease.

The trips I coordinate run smoothly, without error, and are planned meticulously, and it's this particular level of detail when planning, that gets my CEO from A to B to C efficiently, and stress free.

Throughout my 20 year career as an executive assistant, I've learnt not only how to do the job well, and meet the expectations of my line manager, but to go 'above and beyond'. I've learnt how to exceed the expectations required of me, and to deliver beyond the job specification. I practised 'continuous improvement' before it was even a thing!

As executive assistants we have a natural passion to improve things, to streamline processes, and to add structure. We're organised, efficient and meticulous, with a keen eye for detail. We enjoy calendar management, because it's like solving a constantly changing puzzle, and we love a challenge! We focus on the detail, whilst our executive focuses on leading the business, and that's what we enjoy.

Every day throws up a new challenge, a new meeting priority, a shift in focus for our executive, and no two days are the same. We've learnt how to pivot from one priority to another, and we smooth out the bumps along the way.

I've worked across many different business sectors, including legal services, banking, finance, BPO, CX, life science, technology, telecommunications, and most recently a private equity start-up, and **I know that EA skills are transferable across ALL sectors.**

OK, so the terminology and the acronyms may differ from one company to the next, but the role of the corporate EA does not change that significantly. **We ALL do the same core tasks throughout the week.** The core tasks being calendar management, business travel co-ordination, and scheduling meetings. So, no matter what sector you're currently working in, the techniques shared in this book are 100% relevant to you, if you're a corporate EA.

Let me explain the backstory that led me to publish 'Executive Assistant Mastery'. For the past 6 years, I've worked as an executive assistant contractor. Which means I've completed a full time contract for a fixed period (often 9-12 months) with one company, before moving onto the next. Sometimes they were maternity cover roles, sometimes not. It's a path I chose to explore, after many years of committing to permanent, full time, roles.

Working as an EA contractor, for the past 6 years, has allowed me to work in different sectors, for different sized companies, across different geographic regions, and I've supported executives who were based in the UK, US, and Europe, so it's been a massive learning curve.

I've worked for supersized multinationals, with colleagues across EMEA and APAC, and on the flipside, I've worked for start-ups with less than 100 employees across Europe. It's given me variety, an insight into different company cultures, and shown me how many businesses operate.

Introduction

The process of completing a contract, and starting a new one, meant that I was transitioning to a new executive, a new business, and a new operating system every 12 months or so. Repeating that process, made me reflect on what was required as an EA in each role, and what I delivered.

I drew comparisons from each contract position, and I considered the actions I'd completed in the first 30, 60 and 90 days in each role, and I saw a pattern emerging.

If only I had captured this process – I thought! Because for every new contract I start, I'm faced with the same set of challenges. The calendar isn't operating as effectively as it could be, meetings are moving around at short notice, business travel planning is poorly executed, and there are too many meetings being crammed into the workday. I discovered that a lot of existing practices were ineffective, and open for improvement.

To combat these issues, I implemented several of my own EA techniques, to optimise the calendar, transform business travel planning, and revamp recurring meetings. I re-structured calendars, I laid calendar foundations, and I completed calendar audits.

I repeated the process again and again, for each contract role (and each new executive I supported), because my tried and tested techniques worked, and I soon realised that I'd developed a solution to the common problems!

Having reached the conclusion that a process **did** exist, to improve calendar management, business travel, minimise meeting churn, and improve meeting scheduling (no matter who I supported, whatever sector I was in, or how big the company), I thought I'd document the process and share it. I named the process **Executive Assistant Mastery,** and the concept of my new book was borne.

Executive Assistant Mastery

In this book, I'm sharing with you the tools and techniques I use to make the biggest impact to my executives in 90 days. These are the techniques that I've developed, tested, improved upon, and use every day, as an executive assistant.

They are relevant, up to date, and powerful tools, for you to use collectively in your role, and will be hugely impactful to your boss. I've broken the process down into 43 steps, which makes it easier to work through, and implement.

Your challenge is to complete the 43 steps within 90 days. Which is a manageable timeframe, as long as you're committed to the process.

Whilst I can give you the tools, it's up to you to put in the work, and to maximise the impact. Are you up for the challenge? Of course you are! Get ready to show your boss what EA Mastery is all about...

Maria Fuller
Author and Executive Assistant
November 2023

Reader Reviews for 'How to be a PA'

 In Minnesota

★★★★★ **Invaluable Resource for the Administrative Assistant in their Early Career**
Reviewed in the United States us on April 26, 2021

An Administrative Assistant role is something people sometimes land in without knowing what they signed up for and how to do their jobs effectively. Typically there is little training on how an Administrative professional should carry out their day to day duties as a trusted advisor VIP to their Executives.
This book offers an insight and overview and go to guide for Assistants to some of the most important aspects of their jobs.
A highly recommended read for those who are looking for help and guidance and perhaps a little help navigating this career!

Mea Taylor

⭐⭐⭐⭐⭐ **Helpful and insightful reading**

Reviewed in the United Kingdom GB on 15 March 2021

Verified Purchase

I was given this book for my birthday, as I'm about to embark on a new career as a PA.
This book is so helpful, insightful and interesting to read. I've had it a week and I'm almost finished!
I start my PA job in finance next week and this book is going to be part my little "bible" of knowledge. If you're thinking of working in this field or are new to it you should definitely purchase a copy.

 Ms. Helen A. Bawden

⭐⭐⭐⭐⭐ **A really great present to have received!**

Reviewed in the United Kingdom GB on 2 February 2020

I was given Maria Fuller's book as a gift as I recently started my VA business. Previous to that I had been a virtual PA in a very particular industry (music) I was drowning in terminology & the differences between the two roles. Maria's book helped me sort the wood from the trees in a very clear & readable way for which I was most grateful. Although this book is based on PA's in a work place there was invaluable information for me as a VA at home. Thank you so much for writing it Maria Fuller! And thank you to the gift giver that mean't I got to read it!

 Valerie Atkinson

⭐⭐⭐⭐⭐ **Encouragement**

Reviewed in the United Kingdom GB on 21 January 2020

I really enjoyed reading Maria's book on How to be a PA. I felt I was taken step by step along a road which initially felt too daunting to start, but with examples and 'top tips' shared through her own experiences, Maria was able to offer encouragement to me.

 Alessia Serpi

⭐⭐⭐⭐☆ **A complete guide for PA job**

Reviewed in the United Kingdom GB on 15 December 2019

Verified Purchase

Easy reading, good tips and advice. The book I was waiting for for a complete guide for someone like me just started personal assistant profession.
Well presented.

 Josh

⭐⭐⭐⭐⭐ **Fantastic book**

Reviewed in the United Kingdom GB on 2 February 2019

This book was a great help for my daughter who recently entered a PA position, it also is an exiting insight to the inns and outs of this job.

Reader Reviews for 'How to be a PA'

 JP

⭐⭐⭐⭐⭐ **An excellent book for an aspiring PA and for those already doing the job**

Reviewed in the United Kingdom GB on 15 July 2016

Verified Purchase

Oh how I wish this had been available when I was working full time as a PA.

It is an excellently detailed and yet concise guide to being a successful PA. It offers enough hints and tips for those new to the role to enable them to get stuck in, but also handy reminders and tips for those already working in the role. I particularly liked the comment about being able to read minds being a key asset in Chapter 3 - being able to read indecipherable handwriting was also a skill honed over time and it is these kinds of skills that make the difference with a PA. It certainly brought a wry smile when I read that and was the kind of comment that showed the author really does understand the role perfectly. I also found the London chapter very useful.

I purchased it as I have taken on a new role recently that has put me back in an office environment again on a part time basis, 20 years after I was last in one full time. Having run my own business over the last 10 years I'm aware I'm not "office savvy" in the same way anymore. This book has enabled me to brush up on half forgotten skills, and brought me back up to date on new ways of working in office environments today.

 C L

⭐⭐⭐⭐⭐ **Must-read book for all Personal Assistants, Executive Assistants and Virtual Assistants**

Reviewed in the United States US on May 14, 2018

Maria Fuller demonstrates her expert knowledge of the Personal Assistant role in this must-read book for any aspiring or current Personal Assistant, Executive Assistant or Virtual Assistant looking to sharpen her/his skills. As you would expect of a book written by an experienced Personal Assistant, the organization of the content makes it easy to understand and take action. Maria uses icons throughout the book to signal 'Top Tips', 'Add to Bible', and 'Act Now'. When I started my first role as a Personal Assistant many years ago, I had no guidance or training and had to muddle my way through. This book would have made me a more pro-active Personal Assistant much faster. I've been a Personal Assistant, Virtual Assistant and now CEO of my own company, and with all of my experience, I still learned some new things from Maria's book. I remember well that I often felt isolated as a Personal Assistant. My bosses were always appreciative of my work, but it was difficult to benchmark my performance against professional standards for Personal Assistants. 'How to Be a PA' will make sure that you're delivering a gold standard service to the boss that you support.

Amazon Customer

⭐⭐⭐⭐⭐ **Invaluable asset to keep with your bible!!**

Reviewed in the United Kingdom 🇬🇧 on 29 June 2016

Verified Purchase

Very useful tool to have, great info in all areas – very thorough and very logical.
London info esp. useful as I seldom travel to London personally but my peers do frequently.

I have picked up some great tips to enhance my own. Reminder again that every day is a school day!
I have joined a couple of the websites so far, amazing to know how much info is out there (and free)
when you start to look properly.

You seem to be a guru with the PA networking!! I just haven't got the time at the moment to commit
to something like that at this stage in my life.
For someone who is starting out in the industry – invaluable tool for them have, esp. info regarding PA
mentoring!

Reader reviews are incredibly useful. I enjoy reading your comments, and I
know it helps others too. Please consider leaving a customer review for
'Executive Assistant Mastery' on Amazon. You never know, it could feature in
my next book!

Mastery Icons

Inside this book you'll find 'mastery icons', supporting you through the 43 step process. You'll find icons in the following categories:

1. **Continuous Improvement**
2. **Add to Bible**
3. **Timesaver**
4. **Collaboration**
5. **Attention to Detail; and**
6. **Checklist**

Each mastery icon will prompt you to complete a task, build your reference file, work directly with your boss or colleague, use timesaving techniques, or build a checklist. Take a look at each icon, in more detail, below.

Throughout your reading journey, keep an eye out for the **continuous improvement** icons. These icons serve as cues to encourage you to evaluate existing processes and systems, within your organisation. What can you improve upon and how? Continuous improvement icons encourage you to challenge the status quo, and explore better solutions for you and your boss.

 Add to Bible...

Every EA needs a **Bible,** this is a digital file where you keep all your essential information together in one place. I use a Word file for this, and add key information e.g. my executive's travel preferences, how to book meeting rooms at different sites, key contacts at different locations, preferred hotels, and restaurants by city. It's a massive reference file, which I refer to daily. **Add to Bible** icons flag up key points to add to your own EA Bible, for future reference.

10

Discover an array of valuable time-saving strategies tailored specifically for executive assistants. Designed not only to boost your own efficiency, but also to benefit your executive. In our fast-paced professional world, time is a precious commodity, and the **timesaver** tips you'll encounter in this book, will prove to be invaluable assets.

Collaboration is when 2 or more people work together, to complete a task, or achieve a goal. Sometimes our executive assistant default is to work alone, but we don't have to. Microsoft Office 365, and Google Workspace, provide us with collaboration tools, to work effectively with our EA peers, our team, our boss, and our internal stakeholders. Collaboration icons flag up opportunities for you to ditch the work alone ethic, and try out some collaboration techniques for faster results.

Attention to detail is an EA skill that allows you to complete tasks with thoroughness, consistency, and accuracy. When you pay attention to the detail, you'll produce quality work, without error. Using this skill must become your default as an EA. We are detail driven professionals, who strive to produce the highest quality of work, and we set the bar high for others. Look out for these icons when it's time to focus on the detail.

Building a **checklist** for repeat tasks is an efficient way of working. It speeds up the time taken to complete a task, and means you don't forget anything. Checklist icons highlight when a checklist works best, gives examples, and you'll be prompted to build you own, as you move through the steps.

THE 43 STEPS TO EXECUTIVE ASSISTANT MASTERY

1

Productivity Hacks

STEP 1. The 43 Steps

Over the past 6 years, I've competed 6 long term contracts as an executive assistant. Each contract was full time, lasting 9-12 months, supporting either a CEO or a C-level executive. Each Long term contract was effectively like starting a new job.

After the interview and selection process, I went through an onboarding process. I completed inhouse training on company systems and platforms, read up on company policy, and got a handover from my predecessor, if I was lucky.

I studied organisation charts, researched the company's products and services online, and attended new starter webinars. I did everything required of me in order to get up to speed, quickly.

After that I focused on the job. I did what my boss asked me to do, and I kept my head down.

But herein lies the problem. Everything I'd experienced when starting a new EA position, required me to be reactive. Learn this, read that, check out that policy, attend this webinar, join this call. It was all one way information, and I was on the receiving end. The focus was to build my knowledge, learn systems, get up to speed, and that's great, **onboarding is great**, but what happens after that?

Then, you're left to you own devices. You pick up the pieces as the EA, you do what your manager has asked you to do, and you get on with it.

Think about that statement for a moment... "You do what your manager has asked you to do." Now ask yourself the following questions:

1. Is your manager an EA?
2. Has your manager ever been an EA?
3. How many calendars has your boss professionally managed?

4. How many business trips has your boss professionally co-ordinated?
5. Is your boss an expert on business support and administration?
6. When did your boss last complete a calendar audit?

Your boss is not an executive assistant, or a professional calendar manager, or a successful planner of business travel. YOU ARE.

You're the person that's been employed as an expert in this field. You're an experienced professional, and you have a wealth of knowledge to share. You are the executive assistant master – not your boss.

With the onboarding and training out of the way, it's time to stop being reactive and start being proactive. You are going to show your boss what executive support looks like. Your boss can't tell you what it looks like, because he or she doesn't know that, yet.

The 43 steps will give you the confidence and the techniques to make the biggest impact in 90 days. Whether you're new to your role, or well established in a long term position, the step by step process will guide you through the core areas to focus upon.

I know the steps work because I've tested them, in my capacity as an executive assistant, at CEO level. Sometimes I didn't get it right first time around, I made changes, I tried a slightly different method. But the 43 steps I'm sharing with you here, are pure EA gold.

The 43 step process will take you on a journey to EA mastery. It's the process I used and repeated for all of my contract roles, with phenomenal results. It's your roadmap to transforming your bosses effectiveness, and to truly master your craft.

Frequently Asked Questions: The 43 Steps

1. **Do I work through the book methodically or can I dip in and out?**
    The book is designed for you to work through in order, from beginning to end. The content has been structured in a way that groups techniques by category, allowing the reader to become the master of one category, before moving onto the next.

2. **There are 43 steps – can I skip some?**
    The steps have been designed to form a process. Skip a step and you'll miss a key component.

3. **When should I read 'Executive Assistant Mastery'?**
    I strongly recommend you read 'Executive Assistant Mastery' during your workday. Afterall, it's a learning and development book, and your employer is going to benefit. When you learn how to do something, you want to put it into practice whilst the knowledge is still fresh, right? Why would you read a practical book about work, outside of worktime? It makes no sense. Your employer is going to reap the benefits of your learning, so don't feel guilty about learning during work time.

4. **I'm so busy at work, I don't think I'll have time to complete all the steps?**
    Make time. Your self-development is important, and ultimately your boss is going to benefit from your expertise. Block out regular time in your calendar to complete EA Mastery Steps.

5. **Should I read all the steps, then implement them?**
    No, to maximise the ROI of this book, <u>read, and complete, one step at a time</u>. Executive Assistant Mastery is deliberately laid out in a format which allows you to learn and implement techniques, one step at a time. Read the book during your workday, and implement during your workday.

6. How can I achieve the 90 day deadline?

Set yourself a target of 3 steps per week, minimum. That's 1 week to read, learn, and implement 3 steps.

7. Do I need paid for apps or additional plug-ins?

No, all the techniques featured in this book are actionable using the software already at your disposal e.g. Microsoft 365 or Google Workspace. You don't need any additional apps or paid for plug-ins.

8. I purchased this book myself, can I expense it back to my employer?

Most definitely, yes. Make sure you expense back the cost to your company. It's a training resource, they should reimburse you.

Block out regular time in your calendar to read and work through the 43 steps. Invest in your own learning and development, and schedule the time to do it. If something comes up which means you can't use the time for EA Mastery Steps, move the calendar entry to the next day, but make sure you find the time to action it. Investing in yourself is paramount, and 2-3 hours per week to work through the book will be hugely impactful, for you, your executive, and for your career. Do it now, and make a commitment to yourself to complete 3 steps every week.

When you've finished the 43 steps, keep your copy of 'Executive Assistant Mastery' for future use. Because whenever you change jobs, or you're given a new executive to support, you'll be setting up your systems all over again. Revisiting the 43 steps will help you to establish EA mastery quickly, smoothly, and effectively, when you need to get to grips with a new role, or executive.

STEP 2. The Firebreak

Calendar management is something we do every day, for our executives. It's a privileged responsibility to have, because we see exactly what's happening in our executive's calendar, in real time. We see new meetings being scheduled and confirmed, we see meetings moving to new times, and we see urgent meeting requests arriving for later the same day.

There are recurring meetings, and ad hoc meetings. There are external stakeholder meetings, and there are client meetings. There are many moving parts within a calendar, and it's up to us to keep the calendar schedule as organised as possible, by planning in advance, implementing the correct **meeting cadence**, and establishing a **rhythm of business**. *More on those topics later.*

As calendar managers, we also have visibility of what **isn't** working in the calendar. We have direct access to calendars that may be full of bad habits, and poor time management techniques. I'm talking about **meeting overlaps**, **double bookings**, and **declined meetings showing in the calendar** (just in case your exec changes their mind later on!).

Scheduling **back to back** meetings all day, every day, is another **bad habit** that is actually counterproductive. If your executive's schedule consists of back to back meetings, calls, and workshops (with no lunch break) it can be challenging to find space for a new business critical call, at short notice. But we accommodate requests like this because this is what we do. Urgent issues can arise out of the blue, without prior warning, and we must make the necessary adjustments.

The challenge of finding space for an urgent meeting, when the calendar is booked solid, regularly lands at the EA's door, and we do what we can to make things work. Yes, it's going to completely mess up your perfectly structured calendar, which was planned for the day ahead, and it's going to take up your time to reschedule existing meetings, but **calendar management is our skill**. We demonstrate agility and flexibility, and make this happen effortlessly (or at least we appear to do it effortlessly).

When I supported Thomas, a CEO of a London fintech start-up, his calendar was booked solid from 09:00 to 18:00 every day, without any lunch breaks. After a short period in the role, I realised that I was often asked (at very short notice) to move his existing meetings around, to make way for an urgent call the same day. This practice was happening regularly, in fact, almost every day, and I was using all of my pro-active calendar management techniques to prevent this scenario from repeating.

The problem with moving meetings around regularly, to accommodate a new 'urgent' call, is that it has a cascade effect for everyone involved. You move 1 internal meeting (with 4 attendees plus your boss), and that's impacting upon 4 colleagues' calendars.

If those 4 colleagues already have existing meetings confirmed (at the time your proposing for the reschedule) the impact goes even wider. Because that's 4 colleagues moving their own existing meetings out, to make time for your boss and the reschedule request.

What if the 4 meetings, that have to be moved out, have a total number of 4 attendees each? That's 4 original attendees, moving their own meetings out, with each one containing 4 people. That's 16 people having to rearrange their schedules, as a direct consequence. Goodness knows how many people that's affecting further down the line. Do you see the cascade effect it's having?

Its poor time management for everyone involved, and its duplicating work, by moving a meeting out, that you've already spent time on scheduling in the first place. If your scheduling across different time zones, rescheduling a meeting isn't a quick fix. So, constantly moving meetings around, at short notice, is best avoided, wherever possible.

Back to the case in point... I was having regular catch-ups with Thomas, the CEO of the fintech start-up, to anticipate his scheduling needs. I'd regularly finish my workday with the next day's meetings ready to go, and aligned with his requirements. But overnight something would always happen, and the next morning I'd get the same request. "Maria, can you please move the xxx meeting, I need the time back for an urgent call, which I need you to set up."

OK, you expect this to happen now and again, but NOT EVERY DAY. It was like groundhog day, over and over again, and I was determined to prevent meeting conflicts from happening, every single day of the week.

My solution to this issue, was to introduce the 'lunch break' blocker into the calendar, because there wasn't one. I added a recurring series of 1 hour blockers into the calendar, daily, between 13:00-14:00 UK, to break up the back to back meeting habit Thomas had developed, and to allow space in the calendar for anything urgent.

The 'lunch break' blocker was colour coded a different colour from his meetings, and it sat proud in the calendar. The 'lunch break' blocker would also give my exec an opportunity to get something to eat (which had concerned me as he didn't appear to be doing this).

I misguidedly thought my traditional, but basic, solution had fixed the problem. I'd protected a 1 hour gap for anything urgent, and this would reduce the amount of meetings I was moving last minute. Sadly, my solution didn't work.

I soon realised that the 'lunch break' blocker I'd introduced, was being converted into non-urgent meetings by Thomas, who had agreed to them via Slack conversations.

He'd given into the demands of others who wanted his time, and he'd released the 'lunch break' blocker to accommodate them. Unfortunately, with channels like Slack, you can't field every meeting request on behalf of your boss, because meeting requestors bypass you, and go direct to your boss. So, whilst I'd blocked time out for him on a daily basis, he was releasing it for non-urgent calls, via channels I couldn't control.

After observing this practice continue for another week, and still moving meetings around last minute (so I could factor in the urgent meeting requests), I reached the conclusion that whilst I'd offered a solution to the problem, what I hadn't changed was Thomas's mindset. The 'lunch break' entry in the calendar was being ignored, and so it was back to the drawing board.

I reflected upon what had happened, and why my solution had failed. I decided that whilst blocking a 1 hour window was correct, I hadn't positioned it correctly to my boss, in order to secure his adoption. He wasn't a 'go to lunch' person, he didn't observe lunch breaks.

Maybe he thought it was an unnecessary application of his time, in a start-up company where he was under a huge amount of pressure. Maybe he didn't like seeing the subject 'lunch break' in his calendar. Who knows.

I don't give up easily, so I raised the subject again, during my usual 1:1 with him. This time I was better prepared. I'd re-branded my original solution, given it a new name, and I'd prepared numbered points on the issues my solution was going to resolve.

Our 1:1 took place via Zoom, and I shared my screen view of the calendar with him, to demonstrate my point. I explained that I was going to introduce a new concept, into the calendar.

"It's a concept called **The Firebreak**" I said, "and it's going to increase your productivity, your time management, and give you time back for urgent calls during the day".

"The Firebreak works like this" I explained:

1. A new 1 hour time blocker is added daily into the calendar, it's called **The Firebreak**. I'll place it midpoint in your schedule, but it can move around if need be.

2. **The Firebreak** is reserved for your urgent, and business critical calls.

3. **The Firebreak** creates a channel midpoint in your day, it's a buffer.

4. **The Firebreak** provides a hard stop between your AM meetings and your PM meetings. If any of your AM meetings are overrunning, this is the reset button, so you start your PM meetings on time.

5. If **the Firebreak** time isn't required for an urgent call, use it to respond to emails, or to grab a coffee.

My repositioning of the solution went down well, and I had the green light to adopt it, and add it to the calendar, which I did the moment we finished the call.

But did it work? Yes, it was an enormous success! What I didn't mention to my exec, is that it's a concept I created and named myself. Remember, you heard it here first!

Introduce your exec to **The Firebreak** concept. It's a 1 hour blocker in the calendar which remains free of meetings. Encourage your exec to protect it, and use it for unscheduled urgent calls, urgent emails, and **time for firefighting**. It also acts as a **hard stop** in the day in between AM and PM meetings, and will act as a reset button, if any AM meetings are overrunning.

STEP 3. Executive Assistant Bible

I'm not religious, but OMG I would be lost without my EA Bible! I use it daily.
It's the one document I open up on launching my laptop, and it's pinned to my
taskbar. It's not a Bible in the religious sense, an EA Bible is a reference file you
create and update regularly. Like a regular Bible, it becomes your manual,
guidebook, or handbook. It's an indispensable working document for an
executive assistant.

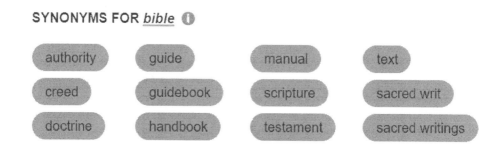

Every time I start a new role as an EA, the first thing I do is create a new Bible.
An EA Bible contains key information, facts, contact details, and links to
frequently used in-house files and templates, relevant to your particular role
and company.

It's your digital directory, keeping key information easily accessible in one place.
Consider it your master document, for collating useful information.

Add to Bible...

Every EA needs a **Bible:** this is a document where you keep
all your essential information together, in one place. I use
a Word file, and add key information e.g. my executive's
travel preferences, how to book meeting rooms at different
sites, key contacts at different sites, preferred hotels, and
restaurants by city. Add whatever information is relevant
to you and your role – it's **your** Bible.

Your EA Bible will grow, as your experience grows in the role. When you recognise your using the same internal files or templates regularly, embed the links to those documents in your Bible. If your regularly viewing the travel and expenses policy, embed the link to the policy in your Bible.

Don't waste time repeatedly hunting around for internal documents, templates or company policies. Let your Bible be your 'one stop shop'. Spending a little time on building your Bible in the beginning, is going to save you heaps of time in the long run. Because every time you discover how to do something in your role, you're going to write up your notes on how you did it, and add it to your Bible.

When you need to complete a task you haven't completed for some time, open your Bible, and view your notes.

The Bible evolves over time, as you develop your depth of experience and knowledge for your role. It grows with you, and every time your improve upon a task, update your Bible on how you did it.

Document how to do repeat tasks like expenses, and add the notes to your Bible. Keep your notes concise and easy to use. Next time you have the exciting task of expenses to complete, use your Bible notes to help speed up the process!

Benefits of using a Bible

Knowledge: An executive assistant is the 'go to' person for their executive. You should have the answers for every question asked of you, in relation to your organisation. You provide the 'one stop shop' of information and nothing is going to escape your memory, or elude you, when you're put on the spot and need to be faster than Google with the result. Building a Bible with all of your knowledge will be beneficial, in finding that essential piece of information when you need it.

Business Travel: Let's say your line manager asks you to plan a new business trip to Boston. You need to research the fastest route possible to Boston, with minimal disruption. You need to locate a hotel close to the meeting venue, or office, and you need to research the transfer, from Boston Logan Airport (BOS) to the hotel. If your manager is staying a while, you'll also need to research suitable restaurants, for any team or client dinners required. In addition, you need to research daily transfers, from your exec's hotel to the office.

Your research is going to take time, and when the trip's complete you should ask for feedback from your exec, to see 'what worked' and 'what didn't work'.

But the most important thing to do with the results of your trip planning, is to 'Add to your Bible'. Add the route flown, which airline carrier you used, the hotel you booked, the type of transfers you booked (car, rail, taxi etc), which company provided the transfers (if you used a private driver). The restaurants your exec liked, the restaurants your exec didn't like.

Next time your exec flies this route – visit your Bible. Review your notes and the feedback you received from your exec, and follow the process. By capturing the knowledge you've gained, the next Boston trip will take less time to plan. Plus, you avoid re-booking the hotel, or restaurant, that your exec didn't like.

Onboarding: When you're onboarding in an organisation, the Bible document becomes the most important thing in your day, because you're building your knowledge from the ground up.

If you're on a call with someone, and they share a shortcut on how to secure meeting rooms at a particular site 'Add to your Bible'. If you're completing a video as part of the onboarding process, and you discover a whole set of acronyms which are used internally, snip and paste via your screen and 'Add to your Bible'. Capture it all.

Add to Bible... I have a Bible from my role at Teleperformance UK which is over 100 pages long. I was EA to the CEO UK for 5 years. We had 27 operational sites, and my CEO was a frequent global traveller. My Bible contains the logistics and preferences for every trip, and every site, he visited. I never repeated my trip research twice. I never had to ask my CEO for the same information twice. Start building your Bible today, it will become your best friend in the workplace, and help you to become amazingly efficient.

What to Include in Your EA Bible

1. Name and contact details for your exec's line manager and their EA (with their locations and time zones)
2. Company HQ site address / entry access / route travelled
3. Frequently visited company-site addresses
4. Travel logistics for all sites (airport / transfer time / preferred hotel)
5. Travel policy guidelines (room rates / class of travel allowed)
6. Contact names of reception teams across all sites, with contact numbers
7. Names and job titles of your exec's SLT (senior leadership team) and their EAs (with their time zones)
8. Key executive assistant names, who they support, their contact numbers and email addresses
9. Traveller profiles for everyone you book travel for
10. Home addresses of people you book travel for (for airport transfers)
11. Airport transfer providers
12. In-house private drivers (if your company has them)
13. Car registrations for people you book airport parking for
14. Screenshots of organisation charts
15. Corporate house style guidelines (fonts, logos)

16. HR team contacts for new starters / onboarding
17. Preferred meeting rooms with video conferencing
18. Tech support people at each site
19. Catering suppliers for each site (external / internal)
20. Meetings requiring 'actions' (if you are producing the actions, what's required, link to folder, notes on circulation)
21. Invoices – how to submit
22. Expenses – how to process
23. Mobile phones – how to order, replace
24. Credit cards – how to process, order new, set up account
25. Business cards – how to order
26. Tech hardware and software – how to order
27. IT helpdesk – how to raise tickets and escalate for priority
28. Who the 'go-to' people are in your internal network e.g. events, marketing, graphics, communications, facilities, finance
29. Dietary requirements of your exec and their team
30. Any family member's names and children's ages, for your exec
31. Children's school details (for term times)
32. Visa & ESTA details and expiry dates
33. Passport details and expiry dates

How to Build Your EA Bible

I use a 'Word' file, and add relevant information as and when it arises. The reason I created this in Word, is so that the content is easily searchable. It doesn't matter that information on 'how to submit expenses' is on page 25, because when I open the document, and hit **CTRL+F,** the navigation field pops up. I type in 'expenses' and it takes me directly to that page. I'm not scrolling through the document, trying to find my notes on expenses.

There's no need to spend ages formatting your Bible, it just needs to be functional, no-one else is going to view it. My Bible is messy. It's built for speed.

When I find a new piece of information, which I know I'll use again, I add it to my Bible. It takes seconds to cut and paste, snip and drop, or type in the new data.

  Use **CTRL+F** to find the information your looking for, in your Bible. It saves time on scrolling.

My Bible has subheadings, so it's not a complete jumble. You'll have information that fits easily under subheadings such as 'Booking Meeting Rooms', 'London Office', 'Catering Suppliers', 'Traveller Profiles', 'Boston Trip', 'Expense Reporting' etc.

Add sub-headings to your Bible and continue to introduce headings as you build it. Add anything that's useful, or you think you will refer to again.

Keep your Bible file secure. It contains confidential and personal information, that must not be shared with others, such as home addresses, passport information, and personal preferences.

Add to Bible... Build your EA Bible. Make it concise, functional, and embed links to frequently used documents and files. Keep it in a secure area on the system and password protect it. Your Bible is a living document, get the basic structure in place today, and add key information to it over the next 90 days.

STEP 4. Your Business Travel Checklist

Yes, you read that correctly **'your'** business travel checklist. This isn't for your boss, this is for you. I've regularly travelled for business purposes as an EA, and those trips often required an overnight stay. When I lived in Bristol, I regularly travelled to work at my company's head office in London, which was 110 miles away. If I had meetings there the following day, I'd book an overnight stay, to maximise my time there.

Now, I live in Devon, and I work for a different employer, but I'm still required to travel to London for work purposes, infrequently. London is 207 miles away, which is a 2.5 hour train journey for me. I also need to factor in additional travel time from London Paddington station to the office (via the tube).

I travel by the fast train with good Wi-Fi connectivity, which allows me to work uninterrupted for the entire length of the journey. There's no downtime to the support I provide to my executive, when I'm travelling for business. I don't sit and watch boxsets, I work. My focus is on my executive, always.

If I catch the 07:25 train, it arrives into London Paddington at 09:55. Allowing for 30 mins to get to Victoria, and a full day in the office, there's little time left to travel back the same day, so an overnight stay is the best option for me.

From my own experience, I've recognised that executive assistants are great at planning business travel for other people, but we aren't particularly good at planning it for ourselves. We put our own requirements to the back of the queue, because we focus on our exec.

However, preparing for your own business journey is just as important, because your role is 'business critical'. Executive Assistants need to function at 100% capacity, and you won't function if you've forgotten something essential like your laptop, charger, or your mobile phone.

Hunting around for items to pack at the last minute, causes stress. Its disorganised, and it can be avoided. Fretting over what you might have forgotten, when you could be calmly walking out of the door, will make you late. Lateness can result in a missed travel connection, which can spiral into travel chaos.

So, in order to prevent your own travel meltdown and to travel like a pro, you need your very own **business travel checklist**.

I created a 1 page checklist to help me prepare for my business trips, and to prevent me from forgetting essential items. My checklist covers off what I need to take with me, plus it helps me plan my outfits.

It also ensures I've covered off some basic home checks, like ensuring the cat is being fed (how could I ever forget the gorgeous Mr Bojangles) and reminds me of all the things I must do before I leave. Like, leaving the wheelie bin, or recycling boxes, out for collection.

 View the business travel checklist on the next page. It's the actual checklist I use, when taking a business trip as an EA. Think about your own business trips. What are the essential items you need to pack? What do you need to do before you lock-up your home?

 Create your own business travel checklist, and save it to your OneDrive or Google Drive. Next time you travel for work, you can either print the checklist, or view it from your mobile device, whilst you pack. Did you miss something? Amend the checklist, get smarter every time you pack.

 Creating your own business travel checklist saves you time, when it comes to packing for your work trip. Sail through the checklist, and you'll pack with confidence. You'll remove the risk of forgetting something, and there won't be any last minute doubts when leaving your home.

My Business Travel Checklist

IT Hardware

- ☐ Laptop
- ☐ Laptop charger
- ☐ Mouse with plug in
- ☐ Mobile phone
- ☐ Mobile phone charger
- ☐ Earphones

Luggage and misc.

- ☐ Travel wheelie bag
- ☐ Across the body bag
- ☐ Laptop soft bag
- ☐ Work notebook
- ☐ Pens and highlighter
- ☐ Business travel or project files
- ☐ Reading book
- ☐ Download podcasts
- ☐ Hand gel

Food

- ☐ Snacks for travel
- ☐ Water

Cat care and house

- ☐ Book cat carer for feeding and leave instructions
- ☐ Kitchen light on timer
- ☐ Household bins / recycling

Logistics

- ☐ Travel tickets (rail)
- ☐ ID
- ☐ Tube ticket
- ☐ Plan route to office
- ☐ Block travel time out in calendar
- ☐ Block any offsite meetings (venues / showarounds)

Personal items

- ☐ Outfits for day
- ☐ Outfits for evening events
- ☐ Shoes (travel flats and heels)
- ☐ Make-up
- ☐ Toiletry bag
- ☐ Hairbrush
- ☐ Vitamins / ibuprofen
- ☐ Underwear
- ☐ Smart coat
- ☐ Slim jacket for train travel
- ☐ Evening bag
- ☐ Gloves / umbrella
- ☐ Tights /socks
- ☐ Jewellery
- ☐ Swimming costume (if hotel pool)
- ☐ Hair band / spray / conditioner

Always prepare the day before. By using the checklist 24 hours in advance, you'll eliminate a sleepless night, wake up confident, and be raring to go!

STEP 5. Identify Your Internal Stakeholders

Executive assistants need to have strong networks around them, in order to complete their roles effectively, quickly, and accurately. The network that's available to you, within your organisation, is a huge resource of knowledge. It's also easily accessible (if you know how), and it's free. Use your network wisely within an organisation, and it will serve you well. But before you tap into that network for knowledge, information, and advice, you need to build your network, strategically.

This exercise is especially critical when you're starting a new role. Your new, you don't know anyone, and it's up to you to put in the groundwork, and build your network. Yes, you may have had an onboarding process, that covers introductions with immediate team members, but you need to cast your net wider.

If you've been in your role a while, don't skip this step. The exercise is still relevant to you, and you'll benefit from refreshing your stakeholder connections.

As EAs we build our own networks for many reasons. Firstly, every EA needs their **'go to'** people, and they reside in many different departments. These are people you 'go to' for support, advice, approvals, and they will become known to you after a period of time. These are the 'helpful' people who'll become a strong resource to you, and help you to get things done.

Secondly, there are **internal stakeholders**. These are individuals within a company, who have a higher level of responsibility. They are 'influencers', and are particularly close to your executive. Finding and engaging with your internal stakeholders is crucial to making things happen, and for that reason we want them on our side.

Identify Your Internal Stakeholders

Identifying and engaging with internal stakeholders, will smooth internal communications for you. Plus, there are many more benefits for EAs. Let's take a look...

Improving your internal stakeholder connections will:

> ➢ Help you get time in the calendar (for your boss), with the stakeholders
> ➢ Speed up responses to any scheduling changes you've proposed
> ➢ Smooth the way for information requests, and approvals
> ➢ Elevate you as the point of contact for your boss
> ➢ Improve your visibility within the organisation
> ➢ Strengthen your internal network

Positive stakeholder relationships are essential, but you have to work at establishing them first, and then maintaining them.

Identify who your internal stakeholders are, before moving onto making connections with them. Your internal stakeholders are going to be the individuals who interact with your executive often, but don't report into him or her.

It could be your boss's peers (someone at the same level/rank), somebody senior to them (their line manager), or a colleague they've worked with closely, on a particular project.

The best way to identify your internal stakeholders, is to access the company's organisation chart. Locate this via your company's internal people platform (e.g. Workday, Bamboo), or via your company's SharePoint or Google Drive.

When you've located your organisation chart, view your executive's position on the chart. Who's equal to them? Who's above them? Which names do you recognise from previous calendar entries, with your exec?

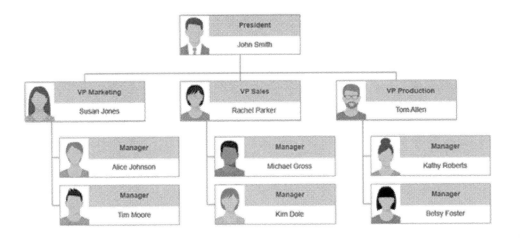

Use the **Snip and Sketch** tool to snip the relevant part of the org chart. Highlight your executive's peers (the horizontal connections on the org chart). Then highlight your exec's line manager (the vertical connection). Save the highlighted version of the org chart to your desktop. The people highlighted are the easily identifiable, internal stakeholders, and these are the people you should reach out to first.

Being proactive when building your internal stakeholder connections, demonstrates that you're focused, and eager to do your job well. Please don't feel that the people you've just highlighted are beyond your reach, or shouldn't be contacted, because they are vastly senior in rank to you. That's simply not true.

You need a reliable network of people around you, in order to do your job well, and to support your exec. Without a strong network, your sabotaging your own success.

When you've identified your internal stakeholders, it's time to reach out to them, and introduce yourself (or refresh your existing connections). But how do you do that, and what should you say? How do you overcome the anxiety, of reaching out to someone really senior to you, in the organisation? Let's find out in Step 6.

STEP 6. Intro Calls with Internal Stakeholders

Working as an executive assistant contractor, for the past 6 years, has given me a huge amount of experience of onboarding, and establishing myself in new roles. I've stepped into the shoes of well-established EAs, who were heading off on maternity leave, on 3 separate occasions.

One role was in banking, one with an investment platform, and one with a tech company. Whilst I received excellent EA handover, and onboarding, in each of those roles, **introductions to internal stakeholders were omitted, every time**.

No EA can perform at their best without a strong network, and that's why it's important to take the initiative, and build connections, with internal stakeholders.

If you've completed the previous step in this book, you've already identified who your internal stakeholders are, by viewing your company's organisation chart. Next, visit your Bible, and under the sub-heading **internal stakeholders,** create a list of the individuals you've highlighted. You're going to use the list to 'reach out' to the individuals, and introduce yourself.

Add to Bible… Create a new subheading in your Bible 'Internal Stakeholders'. Drop the digital copy of your org chart in that section. Below the org chart, insert the names and job titles of the internal stakeholders. Number each entry. You should end up with a numbered list of your internal stakeholders. Finally, insert the date, so you know when the data was accurate. Org charts change regularly, so it's important to revisit this, periodically.

Next, there are a series of smaller steps to complete, before you 'reach out' to the stakeholders. Completing those steps first, will make the process easier, and give you more confidence. It will also maximise the time you have with each individual, during the short 'intro' call, and keep you focused on what to say.

1   Create a spreadsheet called 'Internal Stakeholders'

2   Create column headings titled:
    A. Name
    B. Job title
    C. Reports to
    D. Intro email sent
    E. Call date
    F. Connect on LinkedIn
    G. Questions for call
    H. Call notes
    I.   Actions required

3   Copy and paste the names of the internal stakeholders into column 'A'.

4   Enter their job titles in the adjacent column 'B', and the person they report to in column 'C'.

5   Draft an email with the subject line 'Introduction Call'.* Include a brief introduction of who you are, who you support as an EA, and when you joined the business. Request a brief call (15 mins) and state you'd really appreciate their time. Ask the stakeholder to advise a date and time that's convenient, and offer to issue the calendar invite. Keep the email short, friendly, and professional.

If you've been in your role a while, and are already connected with your stakeholders, think about the last time you spoke to them. When was the last time you had an 'actual' conversation? Swap the email subject line from 'Intro Call' to 'Catch-Up' and ask for a 15 min check-in instead. Complete the remainder of the numbered points.

6   Send the emails individually to the stakeholders. Use the same email text for each stakeholder, just change their email address, and name on the first line. A direct email will have more impact, versus an email sent to multiple recipients at once. Update column 'D' with the date sent.

7   Await the replies, then schedule the intro calls with each stakeholder. Use the subject name 'Intro call: *your name and theirs*'. Keep the calendar invite duration to 15 mins. If you don't receive a reply to your original email, send a follow up email after 3 days. People are busy, they don't always respond straight away.

8   Populate the spreadsheet with the call date, when confirmed. This allows you to monitor the status of your calls.

9   Send a LinkedIn connection request, to the stakeholder. Update the spreadsheet.

10 Prepare questions to ask each stakeholder, and add to your spreadsheet, ahead of time. For example, for a call with the Head of Marketing, I'd ask the questions "Which tradeshows or conferences does the company participate in?" and "Could you please share a calendar of any forthcoming events, that my executive may want to attend?"

For a call with the CFO, I'd ask "Could you please share any financial reporting dates, that need to be visible in my executive's calendar?"

For a call with the Chief of Staff, I'd ask "Are there any specific areas I can improve / focus on, in order to improve my executive's productivity?" or "Can you please share anything that is business critical right now, that I need to be aware of?"

11 During the call, ask your pre-prepared questions, and use column 'H' to record key information, that the stakeholder has shared with you.

12 Finally, use column 'I' to record your own actions during the call. Let's say the Head of Marketing shared an upcoming event with you, that isn't in the calendar. Your action is to add the event to the calendar, and ask your exec if they want to attend.

By building the spreadsheet before jumping on the calls, you've allowed yourself time to prepare, **strategically**.

Think about what information you could uncover, and prepare your questions accordingly. This is an information gathering exercise, as well as an opportunity to build your network. Combine both well, and you've maximised the time you've had with the stakeholders, plus you've left them with a very favourable first impression of you.

Do the groundwork first, before you approach your internal stakeholders. Research who they are, and build a spreadsheet with key data. Think about the questions you want to ask them, prior to the call.

Use the call time wisely. What's the stakeholders job function, and how does that impact on your exec? Target your questions to each individual. If you ask the right questions it will foster collaboration, and strengthen your connections.

Ensure you complete any actions ASAP, and thank your stakeholders for their time, at the end of the call. First impressions count, so be courteous, professional, and keep to your 15 minutes.

Complete all your stakeholder calls within 1 week. Treat it like a mini project. Work through any actions you've given yourself, and embed the link to your stakeholder spreadsheet in your Bible. When you've done that, move onto the next step.

STEP 7. Book Your Office Tour

During the Covid-19 pandemic, everyone shifted to a remote working model. Our new place of work suddenly became the dining room, the spare bedroom, or the end of the kitchen table, which had been cleared of the family clutter. It was a quick fix, which became a 2-year permanent shift, to remote working.

Everyone stopped travelling, which meant that our executives, and their meetings, became 'online' by default. The face-to-face meeting was dead. Online or 'virtual' meetings became the reality, and globally distributed teams were formed.

Since the pandemic, we are much more flexible about our working patterns. Some companies are hybrid, some completely remote with distributed workforces, and some companies (who are really not embracing change) have reverted back to the 'fully onsite' approach. Requiring their employees to be onsite 4-5 days per week, even if they don't have any in-person meetings.

Whichever category your employer falls into, you'll have a central office location or 'hub', in your country, which is used for **in-person** meetings. It's this location that you need to visit, to view the facilities available to your exec, and their immediate team.

Maybe a team member already shared details with you, about the office set up for your company. However, nothing will give you clearer visibility and understanding, than an in-person office tour. Let me explain the importance of an **in-person** office tour…

As an EA contractor, I move companies approximately once a year. I have to build my knowledge quickly, on the resources available to me, and to my executive. When I joined a fintech start-up, I learnt that we were a distributed workforce, with approximately 100 employees based across the UK and Europe.

We didn't have a corporate office HQ to speak of, but what we did have was dedicated space in a shared office building in London, otherwise known as **co-working space**.

Lots of companies are using this model, particularly start-ups, and they lease space from a co-working space provider, such as WeWork, Regus, or The Office Group etc.

Equipped with this information, I researched our London Victoria co-working space online. I read my predecessor's handover notes, on how to book meeting rooms there, and I googled the co-working site to understand the facilities, layout, location, and surrounding area, on a map.

Whilst completing my research online, I viewed images of a calm and serene environment, from which my executive could work undisturbed, in a purpose-built space. I also imagined there were breakout areas he could use, if he had a private or confidential call.

After 12 days in my 'remote' role, I visited our co-working space for the very first time. I pre-booked a tour with the building manager, to maximise my time on site. On my approach, the façade of the building was very impressive. It was a Georgian style townhouse, looking onto a grand square in central London.

However, on entering the building I was completely taken aback by what I found. It was like walking into an overcrowded bar. There were people everywhere! There were multiple queues at ground floor reception, and the noise of people talking was immense.

Upon reflection, it had a great vibe with lots of energy, but it wasn't what I had expected to find, at the headquarters of a financial services company.

The very accommodating building manager showed me around, but when I reached our dedicated office area on the third floor, I was totally shocked by what I saw. The space was tiny. The maximum number of desks had been fitted into the open plan space, to maximise capacity. Each desk only had 1 monitor screen, not the industry standard of 2.

There were no private breakout areas in our dedicated office space. In fact, I realised for the very first time, that there were no meeting rooms (not even a tiny one) in our dedicated area. Nothing.

It was chaos, and not fit for purpose. There were bags everywhere, coats everywhere, cables everywhere, and people were overspilling and trying to work wherever they could perch.

Because there was nowhere for me to sit, I ended up working further down the corridor, at a huge communal kitchen table, with rock hard chairs. Sat immediately opposite, were 2 complete strangers from another company. They were having an informal meeting, and I could hear every word they were saying (the joys of co-working spaces!).

I hadn't been able to pre-book a desk, in our dedicated office space, prior to my visit. In fact, there was no in-house system to pre-book a desk. It was a first come, first served basis, and it was clearly not meeting the demands of the amount of people, who were looking to work there on a daily basis. It wasn't the best, of working environments.

Then suddenly, it struck me like a brick! How had my exec been able to work there effectively? How had he taken private calls? Where had he gone for impromptu 1:1 meetings? How did he 'think' with that constant din?

There were no breakout areas, and no private spaces for calls. I hadn't factored in this challenging office environment, before now. **Big mistake!**

There were meeting rooms available for hire, at an additional cost, but they were located on a different floor to our office. Also you had to pre-book them, to ensure you actually got one. Due to being oversubscribed, meeting room availability was low, and the chance of getting one at short notice, was practically non-existent.

What this experience taught me, was that it's invaluable to complete an in-person office tour, of your company's central office location, **as soon as possible**.

I had no idea our co-working space was cramped, without break-out areas and lacking dual monitors (I don't know about you, but I need dual monitors for calendar management). I had no idea the noise levels were so high that you couldn't think properly, or that you couldn't guarantee getting a desk on arrival.

In comparison to my previous employer (a US tech company), it was the complete opposite of their offices. They had a huge London office with ample space, dedicated breakout areas, and an entire floor of dedicated meeting rooms. They had Herman Miller desks, with matching office chairs, and beautiful soft seating areas. Their offices were professional, calm, and built for purpose. Unbeknown to me, I had been spoilt.

Therefore, I hadn't anticipated such issues with the co-working space of my new employer, and suddenly my eyes were fully open to the situation. I assumed that our dedicated space would be well laid out, with breakout areas, quiet spaces for private calls, and enough desk space to work effectively.

Only an in-person office tour, had demonstrated the many problems to me, and I was thankful I'd made the effort and completed it. But I should have done it sooner, and not 12 days into my employment.

With the office tour over, I knew that in future I had to book more meeting rooms for my exec. I had to plan ahead, and book rooms well in advance. I needed to step up, and combat the issues he was facing on site.

Whether you've got a permanent office, or a co-working space, the importance of completing this exercise is the same. **Book your office tour today.**

Add to Bible... Book your office tour as soon as possible. View everything, meeting rooms, breakout areas, kitchens, café, reception. Add notes to your Bible whilst its fresh in your mind, including how a visitor moves through the building, how do they access your floor. What security measures are in place. How to book meeting rooms etc.

Make connections with the onsite teams at your office HQ. Reception, Facilities, Hospitality, Meeting Room Support, Tech Support and Security. Save their contact details to your Bible. Local connections are vital, Google doesn't always have, all of the answers.

Add to Bible... Embed links or copy and paste into your Bible: onsite catering menus, meeting room layouts, office floor plans, site directions. Build your site knowledge and keep it easily accessible in your Bible. Add the full site address with transport links and nearby hotels.

Don't make the same mistake as me, by delaying your visit. Prioritise your in-person office tour today.

STEP 8. Plan Christmas Gifts Early

When the summer holidays are firmly behind you, and the evenings are drawing in, it's time to start thinking about corporate gifts for Christmas. Traditional corporate Christmas gifts include hampers, food boxes, fine wines, experience vouchers, or anything else your company feels is appropriate to 'gift'.

The majority of companies I've worked for, all send corporate Christmas gifts, to their most valued clients and business partners, and I've personally been asked to own this task, multiple times.

Unfortunately, the process of sending gifts to clients and business partners at Christmas, is often overlooked. It's often left to the last minute. Then, there's a mad panic to find a supplier with stock available, who can ship the goods in time for Christmas.

But, before you even get to the ordering stage, there's a data list of recipients to prepare, addresses to be validated, and a budget to be signed off. You also need to consider your corporate messaging, branding, which logo to use, and personalised messages, etc.

At first glance, planning Christmas gifts seems like a relatively simple procurement task. But beware! Leaving this task at the bottom of your 'to do' list, is going to have disastrous results.

The common mistake with corporate Christmas gifting, is starting the project far too late. Not leaving enough time to plan properly, source suppliers, and ship the goods, is simply bad practice. The outcome is a mad dash to complete the orders, at the time of year when EVERYONE ELSE is doing the same corporate gifting. Which means suppliers are overwhelmed with orders, running out of stock, and couriers are at maximum capacity, resulting in longer lead times.

Rushing the task, is when mistakes are made, clients are missed, and international shipping deadlines are overlooked. It's also worth bearing in mind that December is an executive assistant's busiest month, as we're working on 'annual calendar scheduling' for the following year, and figuring out what adjustments should be made, to improve our exec's productivity and output, for the year ahead.

We're also trying to finish up various admin tasks before the holidays, such as expenses (ours and theirs), and clearing any outstanding tasks before company shutdown. Plus there's Christmas events, parties, team drinks and lunches, Secret Santa, and a whole host of other seasonal things happening, which all demand our attention during the month of December.

Because of the many demands on your time in December, and to get ahead of the pack, I strongly recommend you commence this project in **November**.

By kick starting this project early, you'll avoid the following pitfalls:

1. **Sending gifts to old addresses.** If someone shares the postal addresses with you, from last year's Christmas orders, don't assume the data is accurate. People move house, change jobs, change companies. The recipient data needs to be validated, and that takes time.

2. **Sending gifts to the wrong people.** Just because they were on the list last year, doesn't mean they get a gift this year. Allow time for collaborating with stakeholders, to refresh and approve the recipient list.

3. **Gift items becoming 'out of stock'.** When you're ordering at peak gifting time, suppliers inevitably run out of stock. The closer you get to Christmas, the more their stock levels reduce, and you'll be left with the unpopular gift options.

4. **Late deliveries.** Ordering late could result in missing the suppliers pre-Christmas deadline. A Christmas hamper needs to arrive before Christmas, not after. If a hamper arrives in-between Christmas and the New Year, it's a poor reflection of your organisational abilities, and screams of bad planning.

5. **Stuck in transit.** This can happen if there are issues with delivery carriers. In the run up to Christmas 2022, the Royal Mail in the UK held a total of 7 strike days, relating to pay and conditions. As a direct consequence, mail and parcel deliveries were backed up for weeks.

Raising the question of 'corporate gifts' in November, shows that you're pro-active and organised, and it removes any last-minute panics about who's supposed to be ordering the hampers (or who forgot to order the Christmas hampers!).

Who's responsible for corporate Christmas gifts at your company? If you're new in your role, ask if this is a project you can take-on. Speak to your exec about it. If there's an EA who does this every year, approach them. Ask if you can support, with the Christmas gifts project.

Don't feel you can't put yourself forward for this task. It's often a task that the lead EA doesn't want to do because its time consuming (believe me I know). So an offer of help at the right time, could be well received, and give you an opportunity to lead a project, whist working with senior level stakeholders.

When the project is confirmed, and you know it's your responsibility, ask the right questions to establish your brief:

? What's the total budget?

? How much can you spend per person? Factor in any taxes and shipping costs.

? Who are you sending gifts to (clients/business partners/advisors)?

? Type of gift (food, wine, experience, other)?

? Seasonal (Christmas themed) or standard?

? Branded or non-branded (your company logo or not)?

? Personalised message or standard?

? Deadline for delivery?

? Who holds the data you need? e.g. names, addresses, mobile numbers (courier companies ask for mobile numbers for bulky items like hampers).

? Who will approve the final list of recipients?

With the brief established, you can source your supplier. You may need more than 1, it depends upon the geographical location of your recipients. If all of your gifts are going to addresses in the same country as you (domestic), you only need 1 supplier. If you have a mix of US, UK, and European recipients (international), then split your suppliers by geography.

Place the US orders with a US company, and the UK orders with a UK company, and so on. By choosing **local** suppliers, you'll reduce the distance travelled by the goods, and therefore reduce the associated shipping costs, and delivery times.

When I worked for a biotech company based in Berlin, we used 3 suppliers. One for the UK recipients, one for Europe, and one for the US. It's the most efficient way of sending corporate goods, but it does create 3 X the admin.

Often a project such as this sounds like a quick job, initially. But in reality, it's going to take longer than anticipated, which is why EAs plan well in advance. Add an entry to your calendar for 'Christmas Gifts' in early November to kick start the project.

With the supplier's sourced, complete your data gathering for all of the recipients. Check the integrity of the addresses, and that there are no name duplications. Use a spreadsheet, and add filters for country, category of recipient e.g. (investor/shareholder/client/board member/supplier), and add a column for the relationship manager.

If you're adding a company or personalised message, to each recipient's gift, add a column for that data too.

Share access to the spreadsheet on your company drive, with the internal stakeholders. When the spreadsheet is complete and your happy with the data, ask them to have one final check over the addresses, and the wording of the personalised message. Get the stakeholders/relationship manager's approval.

More and more people suffer with food allergies. If any of your recipients are known to have an allergy, check the contents of the food items you're sending, are safe for them to eat. If in doubt, reach out to your supplier for guidance.

Finally, share the spreadsheet with your exec. Add links to the suppliers, insert the order deadlines, and add a breakdown of costs including price per unit. Ask your exec for final approval.

When you have final approval to proceed (and chase it until you get it), you can complete the order, and work with your suppliers to process it.

Then, with your orders shipped, all you have to do is wait for the 'Thank You' messages to arrive, from the many happy recipients!

Add to Bible...

Update your Bible, with notes on how you processed the Christmas gift orders. Insert a link to the spreadsheet, and the completed order. Link your supplier's website. Add notes on how efficient they were, when managing your order.

The recipients of the corporate gifts will reach out to the person named on the gift card, or their relationship manager, to say 'Thank You'. Make sure those individuals forward any feedback received, to you. Soliciting feedback is about receiving the good, and the bad, comments. If a gift didn't impress, or was received late, you want to hear about it. Feedback will also help you to reach a decision, on who to use, next time around.

2

Business Travel

STEP 9. Your Executive's Hotel Preferences

The majority of corporate executives travel for business, and if your supporting a senior exec in a large company, he or she is probably travelling every week. As an executive assistant, organising business travel, will definitely be part of your role.

Previously, I was employed as the EA to the CEO of Teleperformance UK. That particular CEO, 'Alistair', had responsibility for a business with 10,000 employees, across 27 sites (in the UK, Ireland, and South Africa)..

Alistair was a frequent business traveller. He travelled to multiple sites on a weekly basis, with overnight stays. If the trip was UK domestic, Alistair would often require 1 night's hotel accommodation. If the trip was to the US, he'd stay for 3-4 nights (group HQ was in Miami), and a European trip would be 2 nights. For South Africa, he'd stay for 4 nights in Cape Town (where our largest South African operation was based). The flight duration, from the UK to Cape Town, being a lengthy 11 hours.

Each trip had a full schedule of meetings. Either with internal attendees (onsite), or with a client or supplier (on or offsite). His itinerary would be back-to-back, from his arrival time through to his departure time. There'd also be evening engagements, such as client dinners, team dinners (with the local management teams), or sometimes an industry event.

Whilst it sounds glamourous to travel frequently for work purposes, the reality is somewhat different. Its full on for the traveller. There's no break or rest time during the day, its relentless, and that's just the physical travelling and visiting different locations. In addition, there's the mental energy that's required of your executive.

During the flight, business executives are reading various reports, and studying operational dashboards, in relation to the site they're about to visit. They use their flight time for meeting prep, because once they've reached their destination, they'll be straight into face-to-face meetings and conversations. Traveling executives need to be ready, to dive straight into the detail, and maximise their time, at the destination. They aren't going for a holiday.

So, it's going to be challenging for the executive, physically and mentally, plus there'll be a time zone change to adjust to (if the exec is travelling to another country or a different US time zone).

It's your responsibility, as the EA, to ensure that all business travel and logistics are managed as efficiently as possible, and that includes booking a suitable hotel room for your travelling executive.

Booking **the right hotel,** is crucial to your manager's effectiveness on their trip. It's as important, if not more important, as selecting their preferred seat and cabin class on a flight. The average time spent sleeping in a bed is 8 hours. That's 8 hours of time being either uncomfortable or restless, or sleeping like a baby. It's also the equivalent amount of time spent on a long-haul flight. Think about that for a moment. 8 hours in bed is the equivalent of a long-haul flight. Would you book your boss into economy, for a long-haul flight? I don't think so.

Nobody functions at 100% after a disturbed night's sleep, and you need your executive to be firing on all cylinders. So, ensure you book a great hotel room for your exec, allowing them to rest, and recharge for the day ahead.

Searching online for hotels, can be a bit of a lottery. The travel management platform you're using, will return multiple options, in the online search results. You'll likely use filters to screen out anything 3 star and below, B&Bs, and any low rated customer service providers. Even after applying filters, you'll still be left with a long list of hotel providers to choose from.

Searching for suitable hotels, for every trip, can be time consuming. The quickest route to narrowing down your search, is to **ask your executive for their hotel preferences,** in advance.

They already know the local area, and where they feel comfortable staying. They also have insider knowledge from their colleagues, on the best hotels, bars, and restaurants, within walking distance to the site they're visiting. You only have Google. **Your executive has first-hand knowledge – you don't.**

Let's stop to consider the reality of your knowledge, versus theirs. If you're new, your exec's logistical knowledge will undoubtedly be far greater than yours. He or she will already have visited company HQ (and other company sites) numerous times, and will have experienced the good, and the bad, accommodation providers. **Your exec already knows where to stay, and where to avoid.**

Why would you spend time searching for hotel options, for a location you don't know, when your boss already has the answers. You don't have to complete independent research, when your boss holds the key you're looking for.

 Asking your exec for their preferred hotels for frequently travelled routes, is a no brainer. They know where to stay, and where to avoid. Don't waste time searching online, when your exec already has the answers.

Add to Bible...

 Establishing your exec's hotel preferences, requires a small investment of time, for a long term result. You won't need to ask for their preferences every time they travel. It's a conversation you'll have with them once, when building a trip for the first time. When you've got the information, add it to your Bible, for future use.

When I joined a fintech start-up I supported the CEO 'Thomas', who lived in Germany. His regular travel pattern was Munich to London, work for 4 days in the London Victoria office (stay 3 nights), then return home. I'd received handover from my predecessor, and there were 3x preferred London hotels, listed in the handover document. Thomas's preferred hotels in London were:

Your Executive's Hotel Preferences

1. The Clermont, Victoria, London
2. The Park Plaza, Victoria, London
3. The Doubletree by Hilton, Victoria, London

After 3 weeks in the role, Thomas and I were discussing his next London trip, and what needed co-ordinating.

To ensure the information I held was accurate, I asked Thomas to let me know where he preferred staying, when in London. Thomas replied that there were 3 hotels he usually rotated across, and I should book any one of those. The hotels being The Clermont, The Park Plaza, and The Doubletree Hilton.

To understand his preferences in more detail, I responded with a clarifying question. "Where would you like to stay, if you could choose any 1 of those 3 hotels?" This time there was a pause, then he listed the hotels in the same order as the handover notes.

I was in the process of thanking him, when he interrupted with: "No, wait a minute, this is my preference: first choice The Park Plaza, second choice The Clermont, and if you can't get either of those, The Doubletree Hilton. Also, when you book a room, please make sure I get a King size bed because considering my height *(he is 6' 6" tall)* I need a large bed, otherwise I have to sleep diagonally across the bed. Most importantly, make sure it's not 2 singles joined together, because if I have to sleep diagonally across those, I lay across the join, and that's uncomfortable".

Well, what an insightful response from Thomas! Now I knew his hotel preferences, for when he was staying in London. Plus, he'd alerted me to a problem I wasn't aware of. I knew he was tall, but I stupidly hadn't considered the bed sizes. Poor Thomas! For the past 3 weeks, I'd booked him into standard double rooms, on all of his trips!

But it appeared he had suffered in silence. Thomas hadn't told me of his height issue when I joined the company 3 weeks ago, and it wasn't in my handover notes either. I was so pleased I had unearthed this information, and I was going to put it to good use.

View the image below of hotel bed dimensions. Familiarise yourself with the terms and actual sizes. If you don't see 'King' in the room listing, the likelihood is your getting a standard double sized bed.

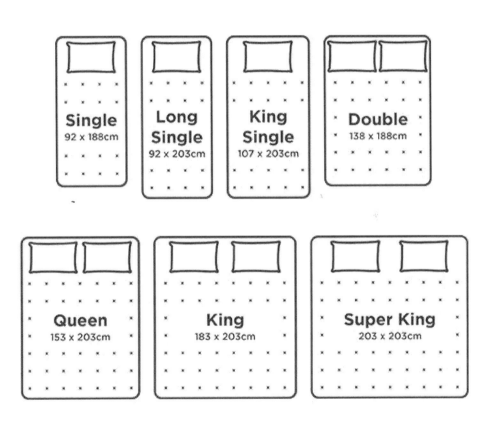

I know you might not be supporting an exec, with a similar height issue to Thomas, but this situation demonstrates why **having a direct conversation with your exec, about their hotel preferences, is invaluable.** Your exec may alert you to something which is essential to their wellness or relaxation, that hasn't been documented previously. Such as a feather allergy, a particular dietary requirement, or a preference to stay at a hotel with a gym or swimming pool.

Work with your executive, to give them the best bedroom options possible. The average sleep time is 8 hours, that's the equivalent of a long-haul flight. If you're regularly factoring in your exec's flight preferences, you should do the same for their bedroom preferences.

Having a direct conversation with your exec, is evidence of your intention to provide a top tier travel service. You're thinking about their personal wellbeing, and planning effectively. They won't know how thoughtful you are, if the only research you complete, is on your own via Google.

Ask about hotel preferences, during your next 1:1 or catch-up call. Pick 1 office or site to discuss at a time, otherwise the conversation could get lengthy. You don't want to drain your exec, or take up too much of their time.

Make sure you get 3x hotel names per location, because you won't always be able to book their first choice. Also, some brands have more than 1 hotel in the same city, so ensure you establish the exact hotel location.

Ask your exec if they're a member of a hotel loyalty programme. Marriott, Hilton, Radisson, Best Western and more, all operate loyalty programmes for guests.

Prepare your hotel questions beforehand, so that you don't miss anything, and keep it conversational. After all, you want your exec to think about their responses, and provide detail.

Add to Bible...

Add all hotel preferences and loyalty programmes to your EA Bible. Start a new section for each location you're researching. Add the city name as the title, followed by the full postal address of the company office. Inset the 3x preferred hotels in order of preference, and embed links to their websites.

When booking accommodation, always adhere to room rate allowances set out in your company **Travel and Expenses Policy**. This is the document which details the maximum spend on hotel room rates, per night. Booking 'out of policy' is to be avoided. The T&E policy may also detail any 'hotel preferred partners'. These are preferred hotels, which your company has secured preferential rates with.

When you've added your executive's hotel preferences to your Bible, it's time to move onto the next step, where you'll research the hotels and build your knowledge for each one.

STEP 10. Research your Executive's Preferred Hotels

So, you've spoken to your executive, and asked them for their preferred hotels. Now you know their #1 choice, plus 2 alternatives. The reason you need to know 3x preferred hotels, is because if the first hotel is fully booked, you can book option 2, and so on.

Availability issues can happen in peak season, as hotels are accommodating tourists, not just business travellers, and if you're trip planning in a popular city destination like London, Boston, or Barcelona, you should always have a backup hotel provider.

My executive confirmed the 3 hotels below, as his preferred hotels, when visiting the London office. This meant I no-longer needed to search and filter all hotels local to the office, every time he flew this trip, I just had to check availability and pricing for 3.

1.   The Park Plaza, Victoria, London
2.   The Clermont, Victoria, London
3.   The Doubletree by Hilton, Victoria, London

That's saving me a considerable amount of time (at the travel planning stage), and providing my exec with continuity (because he knows he's staying in one of his preferred hotels). Whenever I confirm a hotel booking, I use the travel management platform, appointed by my company. Your company will have one too (TravelPerk, Concur, Egencia etc).

With the 3 preferred hotels in the bag, the next step is to increase your EA knowledge of each one, and add the info to your Bible. Completing research for each preferred hotel, will give you a better understanding of the facilities provided, the room sizes offered, the in-room services offered, the leisure facilities, the distance to the office, and the style of the hotel your executive prefers.

The research will give you a feel of the hotel, is it modern, traditional or boutique? What class is the hotel? Is it 4-star or 5-star? Is the hotel a small independent or a multinational chain. Is there a loyalty programme?

By completing your research, and building your knowledge of the preferred hotels, it gives you a greater understanding of what your exec is looking for, and expecting in a hotel. This helps when sourcing hotels in an unknown destination, as you can either find something within the same hotel group, or locate a hotel with a similar design, room specification, and leisure facilities.

Add to Bible...

 View the websites for each preferred hotel. Add brief notes to your Bible on the bedroom options, leisure facilities, loyalty programmes. Are there bars or restaurants on site that might be suitable for future team dinners, 1:1s or coffee meetings?

If the hotel provider is big on event space and meeting rooms, make a note of it in your Bible. You never know when you'll need additional space, for a company event or offsite meeting, and the solution could be to use one of your preferred hotel providers.

View the table on the next page. It shows the notes I created from my own research, into Thomas's preferred London hotels. I also added hyperlinks from the hotels listed in my Bible, to the hotel's websites.

 When adding hotel details to your Bible, create a link from the hotel name to the hotel's website, for easy reference. To create a hyperlink: open your Bible, highlight the hotel name, right-click, click 'Link' on the shortcut menu, add the hotel website address to the address field. Check the hotel name is featured in the 'text to display' field, click ok.

London Office

84 Eccleston Square, Pimlico, London, SW1V 1PX

THOMAS'S PREFERRED HOTEL PROVIDERS		
1	Park Plaza, Victoria 239 Vauxhall Bridge Rd, Pimlico, London, SW1V 1EQ	Walk time to office 3 mins Executive Room Double (King size bed) Size of room 20m2 Sky TV included Room service **Onsite:** TOZI restaurant and bar (Italian) small plates and cocktails (would suit SLT) VIC's Bar: lounge bar with cocktails and all-day snacks (good for coffee meetings) Gym, sauna, steam room Loyalty programme: Radisson Rewards Next to Victoria Station and Gatwick Express Style: Corporate hotel Suite of meeting rooms
2	The Clermont, Victoria 101 Buckingham Palace Rd, London, SW1W 0SJ	Walk time 5 mins Deluxe King or Classic King Room size 26m2 or 20m2 Smart TV Room service **Onsite:** Tea Lounge, The Soak (Restaurant and Bar) Loyalty programme: own Next to Victoria Station and Gatwick Express Style: Grand hotel for tourists and families
3	DoubleTree by Hilton 2 Bridge Place London, SW1V 1QA	Walk time 2 mins King Premium Deluxe (King size bed) Room size (not visible) Room service **Onsite:** Bar and Restaurant Fitness centre Loyalty programme: Hilton Honors Next to Victoria Station and Gatwick Express Style: Corporate hotel Suite of meeting rooms

See how I've added the full address for each one. This is useful when booking ground transfers, I can just copy and paste the address into a booking field. I add walk time, so I can block that out in the calendar, if need be. As well as catering facilities, room service options and leisure, I add the closest transport links. This reminds me what's available, when I'm planning the airport transfers, or any other logistics in the area. I research each hotel once, and record the data.

Most of this information will be available on the hotel's website. Another way to research your executive's preferred hotels for frequently flown trips, is through the eyes of a legitimate hotel guest. EAs don't often get the opportunity to visit preferred hotels and ask for a show around, so the next best thing is to search YouTube (for hotel review videos), and hit play.

Ensure you only play the most recent 'hotel review' videos, because you want your research to be as up to date as possible. Hotels change ownership often, and so do their service levels, so bear this in mind and look for recent and relevant content only.

The benefits of viewing hotel reviews on YouTube, is that you're seeing 'the real deal', and not just the corporate professional video, the hotel has commissioned. A commercially produced video of the hotel's interior, for PR purposes, will only show the hotel looking at its best. A hotel guest's video will give you a more realistic view, without the gloss.

Real customer videos can sometimes offer excellent tips such as: the best public transport options, where the nearest supermarket is (for any urgent items your exec might need) and feedback on in-house restaurants or room service meals. Also, you might learn if there's an issue with street noise, bad service, or slow check-in/check-out times. It's like Trip Advisor, but with video.

Use Google Maps, to discover the walking distance from the preferred hotels to the office. You could even create your own image of the 3x hotels in relation to the office, and add that to your Bible for future reference. Understanding the walking distance, from the hotel to the office, will help with calendar scheduling and blocking out the 'walk to office' time, in your exec's calendar.

View the screenshot below. The large dot indicates the office location. The 3x London preferred hotels are highlighted on the map. This helps to visualise the proximity of the preferred hotels to the office.

London Office 'Preferred Hotels' Map

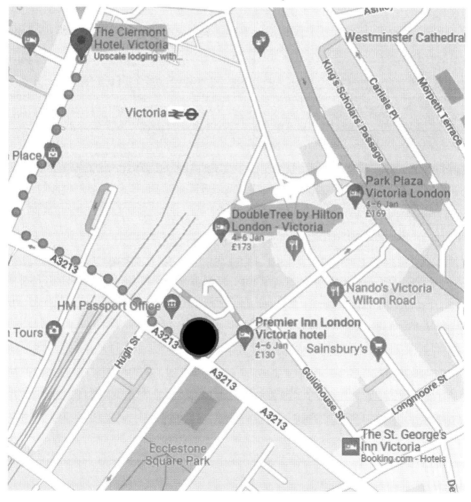

Research your exec's preferred hotels, and build your Bible with useful info. Do this once for each trip, and you'll soon have a library of trip information available to you.

Is your exec staying in the same hotel regularly? Reach out to the hotel team, and introduce yourself. Build a rapport with a reception or reservations team member, located at the hotel. Direct connections can be useful for any late checkout requests, or meeting room hire enquiries.

When a trip's flown and your exec is back at base, ask them for their hotel feedback. Drop it into a conversation next time you speak to them. A simple "How was your hotel, did you sleep ok?" is usually enough to prompt your exec to think about it, and give an honest answer. This should unearth any issues, e.g. there was a check-in delay, the room wasn't to their standard, or the bed was uncomfortable. Update your Bible with any issues reported, so you can avoid them next time around.

With your research complete and your Bible updated, move onto the next step.

STEP 11. Business Travel Glossary

There are numerous acronyms and abbreviations in use, within the business travel industry. Familiarise yourself with the terms and acronyms below, to increase your understanding, and to improve communications with travel industry specialists.

Travel Term or Acronym	Definition
Airbnb	Airbnb is an online marketplace that connects people who rent out their homes, with people looking for accommodation.
Airline Alliance	An agreement between many airlines to work together, to share flying routes and resources, and extend benefits to each other's frequent flyer programmes.
Airport Code	A 3 or 4 digit code for each airport location e.g. LGW (London Gatwick)
Airport Terminal	A building within an airport where passengers go to depart on a flight, or the building at which they arrive upon landing.
Airport Transfer	The transport your traveller is using, to and from the airport.
B&B	Bed and Breakfast
BAR	A Best Available Rate is the lowest possible room rate available on a given date.
Blackout Dates	Specific dates set by an airline, hotel, or car rental agency when special discounts, promotions, or use of miles are not permitted.
Boarding Pass	A document (hard copy or digital) that gives a passenger permission to board the plane. It confirms the passenger name, air carrier, flight date, time and

	number, boarding time, and seat assignment for that flight. Only available once online check-in is complete.
Booking Reference	A booking reference, sometimes called a reservation code or confirmation code, is an alphanumeric code of 6 characters. It uniquely identifies a specific flight reservation within an airline or travel agency's system. It's used for accessing and managing a booking. Passengers can use the code to check in online, make changes to their reservation, or view their booking details. A booking reference code is the same code as the PNR (Passenger Name Record).
Business Class	An airline class above economy (and premium economy), with upgraded amenities, service, and seating.
Carry-On Baggage	A piece of luggage that can be brought on board the plane and stowed in the overhead locker or under the seat in front.
Checked Baggage	Luggage that goes in the cargo hold under the plane during the flight, also known as 'hold' luggage.
CNR	Corporate Negotiated Rate. These are discounted room rates which are usually negotiated between the hotel and the company.
Codeshare	An agreement between 2 or more airlines which allows 1 carrier to market and collect payment, for a flight operated by another carrier.
Connecting Flight	When a flight itinerary requires a traveller to change planes, the flights are called connecting flights.
DDR	Day Delegate Rate, or DDR, is a charge by a venue per person or attendee, for a full day's meeting or event. Depending on the venue, DDR can include meeting room hire, refreshments, lunch, and conference equipment. It's a set price for a package of services, instead of being charged separately for each item.

Direct Flight	A direct flight is any flight between 2 locations. But it may (or may not) include 1 or more stops. It might stop to get new passengers (or allow some to disembark) or for refuelling.
Domestic Flight	A domestic flight is one that takes place entirely in 1 country. The departure and arrival cities are in the same country.
Economy Class	A cabin class that offers passengers the lowest ticket price available.
ESTA	Electronic System for Travel Authorisation, used to determine the eligibility of visitors who travel to the United States under the Visa Waiver Programme.
Expense Policy	Rules created and enforced by companies that employees must observe for business and travel costs. A policy sets out maximum allowances, class of travel allowed and how to reclaim any personal costs incurred.
Expense Reimbursements	Compensation paid by a business to employees that incur cash or personal card expenses, on behalf of that company.
FFP	Frequent Flyer Programme. A loyalty programme offered by an airline to its passengers.
First Class	A category of luxury seating on a plane that has more space, comfort, and service, with amenities ranging from private suites to access to on-board showers.
Flight Number	A flight number is a unique code for a specific flight. It typically consists of an airline code (2-3 letters) and a numeric portion (1-4 digits). For example, BA123 is a flight operated by British Airways.
GDS	A Global Distribution System (GDS) is a computerised network used in the travel industry for booking flights, hotels, and other travel services worldwide.

Ground Transfer	A transfer from one place to another (typically to and from the airport) using anything land based e.g. taxi, private driver, bus, train, or shuttle.
Ground Transportation	All transport options over land, instead of by air or water.
HBO	Hand Baggage Only
Hold Luggage	Luggage that you check-in / leave at bag drop, for storage in the hold of an aircraft instead of carrying with you, as hand luggage.
Hotel Chain	Large groups of hotels e.g. Marriott, Hilton, Radisson, Best Western etc.
HUB	Hub airports are airports that serve as central transfer points, from which flights come in and go out to other cities.
HROT	Hotel Room Occupancy Tax. A hotel tax or lodging tax is charged in most of the United States, to travellers when they rent accommodation.
IATA	International Air Transport Association, a professional association for many of the world's airlines.
Inbound	A flight arriving at the airport
Indirect Flight	A flight with at least one stop
Layover	A layover is a short period of time between connecting flights. On domestic flights this refers to stops of 4 hours or less. For international flights, this refers to stops of less than 24 hours.
LH	Long-Haul. Any flight longer than 6 hours is considered a long-haul flight. These are usually international flights.
Low-Cost Carrier	Also called low-cost or budget airlines. Airlines that have fewer amenities and cheaper prices than traditional full service airlines. EasyJet, JetBlue, and Ryanair, are all low cost carriers.

LNR	Locally Negotiated Rate is a rate negotiated between a hotel and a company.
LRA	Last Room Availability is a negotiated contract between a company and a hotel. It guarantees that the hotel will sell their rooms to the company at the contracted price, regardless of how many rooms are left.
MI	Management Information
Multi-City Flight	A flight with multi-city destinations e.g. from LHR to CDG to DUB. A multi-city flight doesn't follow the normal route of 'there and back again'.
Non-Refundable Ticket	Non-Refundable Tickets in their most basic sense are "final sale" airline tickets that cannot be returned for a refund after purchase.
Non-Stop Flight	A flight with no stops enroute to a passenger's final destination.
Non-Transferable	A ticket that can only be used by the person who was originally scheduled to fly.
OCC	Occupancy
OTM	Online Travel Management
Outbound	A flight departing from the airport
Per Diem	Instead of submitting itemised expense reports for each trip, an employee could claim the Per Diem allowance, which is a daily expenses rate set by the employer (if applicable). There is less paperwork as receipts aren't required.
PNR	A Passenger Name Record (PNR) is a comprehensive record that contains detailed information about a passenger's itinerary, including flight segments, seat assignments, contact information, meal preferences, and more. It's used to store and manage a passenger's entire travel reservation. A PNR may include info related to other travel like hotels and car rentals,

	depending on the booking. The PNR is the same code as the booking reference.
Premium Economy	Premium economy is the class between economy class and business class. The amenities can vary widely depending on the airline and the aircraft, but generally, it's an upgraded experience from economy.
Private Driver	An executive car service providing airport transfers, and an option for meet and greet services (with name board) in airport arrivals.
RO	Room Only. There are no meals included in the rate. Breakfast will be charged on top, if required.
Room Rate	A room rate is the price charged per night for each room category at a hotel, from standard rooms to deluxe suites. Rates are determined by a property's operational costs, competitors, local market, and season.
Rack Rate	The hotel rack rate (or walk-in rate) is the price that a hotel charges for a room before any discounts have been applied. Sometimes referred to as the published rate and usually set artificially high, so that discounts look generous by comparison.
SBT	Self-Booking Tool. The self-booking tool or SBT is an online travel booking software (platform) that corporate business travellers use to plan and book their trips. A self-booking tool helps simplify business travel and accommodation for employees.
SH	Short-Haul. Typically, a short-haul flight is any direct or non-stop flight that flies anywhere, in under 3 hours.
Shuttle Service	Transport that runs frequently between 2 places e.g. an airport shuttle bus, the hotel shuttle bus, or monorail shuttle between airport terminals.

T&E	Travel & Expense Management is the process of controlling the business travel budget by the company. All companies actively monitor travel and expense costs and produce a T&E policy, setting out business travel and expense guidelines for employees to adhere to.
TMC	A Travel Management Company is a company that specialises in corporate travel. A TMC will provide users with a platform for self-booking, and online agents to support with complex booking queries. A TMC captures all booking details, facilitates approvals, and provides financial reporting to the client.
TSA PreCheck	This is a US government programme that allows travellers deemed low risk by the Transportation Security Administration (TSA) to pass through an expedited security screening at certain US airports. Only available for US citizens and US nationals.
VAT	Value Added Tax (UK) also known in some countries as a goods and services tax. Is a tax added to hotel rooms at 20% (and many other goods and services). It is reclaimable by companies which is why VAT receipts are required to accompany expense reports.
VISA	A Visa is an official document that allows the bearer to legally enter a foreign country. Visas should be applied for well in advance, of any business travel.

If you regularly book travel and accommodation for your executive, its essential to learn the correct terminology. Understanding the phrases and acronyms used by booking agents, will ensure that you communicate clearly with each other and that all of your booking requirements are understood.

Learning a whole load of travel phrases in one go isn't easy. My advice is to break the task down into bite sized chunks. Choose a section of the business travel glossary and highlight it. Use as many of those terms as possible this week. Try to use them in an email, in a Slack message, in a chat with your business travel agent, or during a direct conversation with your exec.

The more you use business travel terms, the faster they will stick. Or write some down on post-it notes and stick them to your monitor. Add a new entry into your calendar every week, to learn (and use) 5 more business travel terms. Soon you'll be communicating like an industry expert!

STEP 12. Fast Track Security

Airports can be time consuming to travel through, and your executive can often spend the majority of their time queuing at various checkpoints, before they reach their departure gate.

A fast track security pass enables the traveller to pass through airport security faster, bypassing the normal queues, and stepping into the fast track security lane instead. This eliminates not only the amount of time queueing, but also the associated stresses or complications that can occur.

Imagine its peak tourist season, and your super stressed exec is already late arriving at the airport, due to being stuck in traffic. You've already completed check-in online, but your exec is now 15 mins behind schedule, and time is of the essence. He or she, still has to walk from departures through to security, queue for the security checks, and get to the gate in a reasonable time.

On arrival at security the queue is enormous. There are large family groups and it's taking twice as long to get everyone checked through. Your exec is now getting worried by the queue time ahead, and is feeling anxious about making their flight!

Passing through security is also 'dead time' at the airport. Your exec can't take a call or join a Zoom meeting, as physical and personal items like laptops and mobile phones are going into trays for security screening. They're waiting to be searched, X-rayed, or asked to unpack a bag.

This scenario or 'nightmare' is often a reality at airports, and it's something travel co-ordinators don't experience first-hand, very often. Even if you've allowed plenty of time at the airport, this step can still be stressful and challenging for your exec.

Whilst the security checks are unavoidable, **the main queue _is_ avoidable,** if you purchase a **fast track security pass**.

This 'golden ticket' allows your exec to breeze past everyone else, bypassing the normal queues, dodge the screaming baby or the crying child, and make it safely through security to the terminal departure gate, with their sanity intact. A fast track pass allows the bearer to use a signposted priority lane, allowing them to pass through security faster.

This golden ticket will get you brownie points, if you introduce the concept to your executive. It elevates your traveller from having to pass through airport security with the general public, and gives them a quick and efficient shortcut through a stressful procedure.

For the frequent flying executive, I purchase a fast track pass as standard, wherever possible. It's part of my travel co-ordination checklist. I want to ensure that my exec is going to reach their gate on time, by the quickest route available, and with the least amount of stress.

Fast track passes can be purchased from the airport's website in advance (or at the airport). So, when booking the trip, this is another travel 'extra' to add on. Not every airport offers this service, so you'll need to check with the departure airport if they do. For UK airport departures there is a great website: **holidayextras.com/fast-track,** and this consolidates most of the fast track information for the UK. See the screenshot on the next page.

Fast track passes are inexpensive because they can only be used once, on the date of travel. A fast track pass enables the pass holder to enter a priority lane, which will be signposted at the airport, and skip the queues at security screening. This means your exec will reach the security search-area quicker, and it allows them more time to get a coffee, a bite to eat, or make a phone call before the flight.

A fast track pass is a convenient way to expedite the security screening process, and saves time at the airport. The average fast track pass shaves 20 mins off the security queue for your exec. For a small outlay of £6 that's 20 mins of time back for your exec, which is an excellent return on investment. That's 20 minutes of time that can be utilised for an urgent business call, catching up on emails, or calling home to tell the family they're on their way.

Add to Bible...

Check if a fast track pass is available to purchase at your exec's most frequently used airports. Embed a link in your Bible to the website page where they can be purchased online.

Stand alone Fast Track Passes	
Airport/Fast Track Pass	**Price per person*** **(booked in advance)**
Aberdeen Airport - Fast Track Security Pass	£4
Bristol Airport - Fast Track Security Pass	£6
Bournemouth Airport - Fast Track Security Pass	£3.50
East Midlands Airport - Fast Track Security Pass	£5
Edinburgh Airport- Fast Track Security Pass	£6
Leeds Bradford Airport - Fast Track Security Pass	£5
Liverpool Airport - Fast Track Security Pass	£4
Luton Airport - Security Control Fast Track	£6
Manchester Airport - Security Fast Track (T1, T2 & T3)	£5
Manchester - Passport Control Fast Track	£5
Newcastle Airport Security Fast Track	£6
Stansted - Security Fast Track	£7
Stansted - Passport Control Fast Track	£7

*Please note: These prices are accurate at the time of writing and are subject to change.

Next time your booking a trip, offer to book a fast track security pass. Explain the cost and the benefits to your exec. Is your exec an EasyJet Plus member? If so, fast track security is already included for EasyJet Flights. Check if your exec is aware of this, and is using the member benefits.

Copy Fast Track Pass for LGW

Gatwick Airport

Order No.
DW04081575THO

DW04081575THO

Item in this order

Premium Security

Upon arrival, make your way to the Premium Security lane located to the left of our standard security area and present your order confirmation to gain access.	Date	Qty.	Terminal	Price
	Wed 10 May 2023 16:00	Adult · x 1	North Terminal	£5.00

Order Subtotal:	£5.00
Order Total:	£5.00

Net Price: £4.17 VAT: £0.83 (20%)

The fast track pass is a downloadable 1 page digital file (see above), which can easily be uploaded to your exec's calendar. It contains the date, airport details and a QR code to present at the fast track entry barrier. When you purchase a fast track pass, download it, and add to your execs calendar, for the approximate time they need it.

Not all fast track passes are available from the airport. Some can be added onto the flight ticket, either at the point of booking, or when completing online check-in. Some airports don't operate a fast track line, but if they do have one, your exec will certainly benefit from using it.

STEP 13. Frequent Flyer Programmes

All business travellers love to collect air miles when they fly, and why wouldn't they? It's the equivalent of earning points for the supermarket shop, which can be redeemed at a later date. Except on this occasion, they're not paying for the equivalent of the supermarket shop, their company is.

A frequent flyer programme is a loyalty scheme, offered by most airlines for their passengers. Typically, the airline's customers enrol in the programme, to accumulate frequent flyer miles (or points), which are earned depending on the distance flown per flight. The Miles (or points) can be redeemed for various rewards, including free flights, upgrades to a superior cabin class, lounge access, priority boarding, and more.

It's likely your exec will want to use their accumulated miles to purchase personal travel, a family holiday, or convert their points into flights for immediate family members to use. (This is what my execs have done previously).

Any miles earnt, are an added benefit to the travelling exec. Therefore, they are keen to accrue miles on every trip, so they can enjoy the rewards at a later date. Which means it's up to you (as booker) to make sure their membership number is added to each flight reservation, at the point of booking.

Because frequent flyer miles are earned on potentially every flight you co-ordinate, you'll need to find out which frequent flyer programmes your exec is a member of. You'll need details of the programme, the card number, and the airline alliance.

 Ask your exec to share details with you, for their frequent flyer memberships. The programmes your exec will have signed up to, will be the programmes operated by the airlines they fly with the most.

Each frequent flyer programme will be part of a wider operating scheme, and these are called **airline alliances**. An airline alliance is an agreement between a number of airlines to work together, instead of against each other. Basically, airlines that have signed up to a particular alliance, agree to collaborate with other member airlines in that group, and that's good news for customers.

The 3 main airline alliances are:
1. **Oneworld**
2. **SkyTeam**
3. **Star Alliance**

If your exec has tasked you with booking a multi-city route, sticking with one airline alliance for the entire route is a lot easier for him or her (as the passenger) and for you (as the booker), because the flight reservations, flight connections, and baggage transfers, are far simpler. All the carriers are working together to connect 1 booking, seamlessly (as one airline alliance).

Are you familiar with the term **codeshare**? It's a direct example of 2 or more airline alliance members, working together to operate 1 journey. Instead of working with multiple airline carriers for a multi-connection ticket, you can book as 1 trip, through 1 provider, which is called a 'codeshare'. Airline alliances also make earning (and redeeming) points easier, for travellers who fly across the member's airlines.

An example of a multi-city route using an airline alliance, is from London to 3 major cities in the United States. Say your exec departs from London Heathrow Airport and is travelling to New York City, then onwards to Chicago, and finally to Los Angeles. Here's how it works using the Oneworld alliance as an example:

1. London (LHR) to New York City (JFK) - operated by British Airways, a Oneworld member.
2. New York City (JFK) to Chicago (ORD) - operated by American Airlines, another Oneworld member.
3. Chicago (ORD) to Los Angeles (LAX) - also operated by American Airlines.

These flights are part of the Oneworld alliance, which allows you to book the entire multi-city journey as one transaction, and your executive enjoys the benefits of alliance travel.

The benefits of using an airline alliance are:

- ✓ A single itinerary for all flights.
- ✓ Earning miles across all flights.
- ✓ Lounge access with Oneworld at all airports enroute.
- ✓ A co-ordinated schedule, which means the operators have worked together to schedule flight times, that work for this route.
- ✓ Seamless baggage transfers from one flight to the next. Your exec does not have to re-check bags in, even when they are changing flights.
- ✓ Continuity, your exec knows what standard to expect across the route, as all flights are under the Oneworld alliance.
- ✓ Easier re-booking. Should you get a last minute request to move the date of travel, it's going to be much easier to rebook it.

The alternative is to book 3 flights, that aren't under the same alliance. You're going to deal with 3 sets of booking references, 3 online check-ins and your boss has 3 lots of baggage check-ins and collections to deal with. Its best avoided.

If your exec flies LHR to JFK on a regular basis, and usually flies with British Airways, they'll have a frequent flyer membership with BA. BA's frequent flyer membership programme is called 'executive club'. Members collect 'Avios' points (same thing as miles) when they fly with BA.

There are 4 tiers within that FF programme (blue, bronze, silver, and gold) and members move up the tiers, as they accrue more Avios points. Each tier grants the FF member a different level of benefits.

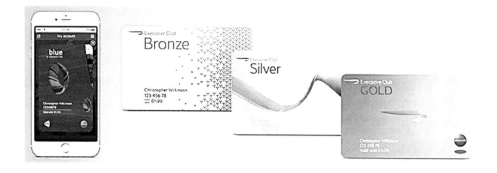

Now, because BA is part of the Oneworld alliance, your exec will also earn Avios points when they travel with any of the other airlines, within the Oneworld alliance network e.g. American Airlines and Cathay Pacific. *See the Airline Alliances image on the next page.*

Avios points are redeemable for flights and other services with BA, and all the other airlines within the Oneworld alliance. Your exec may also benefit from collecting points with hotel partners, who are part of the Oneworld alliance. Marriott, IHG, Hyatt and Shangri-La hotels, are all part of the Oneworld alliance.

If your exec is a global traveller, they'll probably have multiple frequent flyer memberships, and are accruing miles or points across all 3 of the airline alliances. Aside from earning points to use for future personal trips, there are other benefits your exec is entitled to, such as simplified check-in and baggage handling, and priority airport check-in and boarding.

Most airlines offer a separate check-in desk for frequent flyers, and members are usually called to the flight first. However, this is dependent on the airline and departure airport.

Add to Bible...

Add your executive's frequent flyer memberships to your Bible. Ask your exec to send images of the cards over to you for quickness. Which airline alliance is visible on your exec's frequent flyer membership cards?

The 3 Airline Alliances and their Members

Upload your exec's frequent flyer membership details to your travel management platform, under their traveller profile. Whenever you book flights for them in future, the frequent flyer membership number will pull through to the booking, and your exec will earn miles automatically. But you should check this is happening for each flight.

Always ensure that frequent flyer numbers are being pulled through into a flight reservation at the time of booking. Confirmation of this will be visible on the flight confirmation, check that when you receive it. If this information is missed, it means your exec isn't earning points on their flight, and that's a wasted opportunity.

It can be an administrative nightmare to add FF membership details once the booking is complete, so adding the details to your booking platform (to the traveller profile) reduces the risk of the details being missed, and keeps your exec happy. Speak to your TMC to automate this process.

WARNING: miles and points expire. Check the balances of all your exec's frequent flyer miles, on a quarterly basis. They'll need to share their login details with you. Create a spreadsheet showing each frequent flyer programme, airline alliance, total number of points, and the expiry dates. Share it with your exec. Add a reminder to your calendar of the points' expiry date, and prompt your exec to use the points before they expire.

One exception to the airline alliance rule is the low cost carriers (like easyJet). They don't participate in any of the 3 alliances, because they operate on a low budget. However, most of them operate their own membership schemes.

EasyJet's inhouse frequent flyer 'club' is called easyJet Plus. For an annual fee of £125, the member (the frequent flyer) can access dedicated bag drop, speedy boarding, complimentary allocated seat booking, inclusive fast track security, additional cabin bag, and other benefits.

For the frequent easyJet flyer, purchasing an annual 'easyJet Plus' membership is a no brainer. Booking your exec's seat in the extra legroom or upfront area in the cabin, is free for all trips. Check out their website for full benefits, and how to purchase.

An important benefit of frequent flyer membership (with the airline alliances) is access to executive airport lounges, and we'll look at that in more detail, next.

STEP 14. Airport Lounge Access

If your exec is a long-haul flyer, they'll need lounge access at the departure airport. Long-haul flights usually require a minimum of 2 hours check-in at the airport, before the flight departure time. So that's 2 hours of wait time, before the flight time.

This might be a nice problem to have if you're an infrequent flyer, travelling for leisure or the holidays. It gives you 2 hours of retail time, or time to try out the various restaurants and bars, the airport has to offer. **But for the frequent flyer and the business traveller, 2 hours wait time at the airport can be dead time.**

We've all experienced the lengthy wait times at airports, the waiting around on really uncomfortable seats, with no sign of an electric socket to plug your mobile phone or laptop into. It's not ideal, and it can be even more frustrating if there are no seats available, because of flight delays.

However, for business travellers the wait time is even more challenging because they're lugging carry-on bags around with them. They can't leave bags with a colleague or friend whilst they pop into a retail unit, because they're mostly travelling solo. Carry-on luggage has to go to the toilet with them, to the bar, to the restaurant or café.

Plus, if your exec wants to work on their laptop, they have to figure out where to sit that's got a good Wi-Fi signal, within reach of a power socket, with a reasonably comfy chair, and a flat surface for their laptop to sit on. It can be incredibly challenging for them!

Imagine you're an exec going through the same experience after a stressful day, with 50 emails to read and reply to, and an urgent phone call to make. **Stress levels can go through the roof when travelling, so pre-empt the stress for your exec, and consider lounge access at the airport.**

For a short-haul flight, I personally don't think you can justify the additional cost of lounge access, as travellers don't really have time to reap the rewards. But for anyone travelling long-haul, with 2 hours or more to kill at the airport, it's a no brainer.

Accessing a lounge at the airport, can provide the executive traveller with a host of benefits, including:

1. **Comfort:** a quiet and luxurious environment with comfortable seating.

2. **Productivity:** a work area with laptop space, charging points and Wi-Fi connectivity.

3. **Sustenance:** food and beverages (including alcohol) may be complimentary (check the lounge provider). Catering options range from cold buffets to fine dining.

4. **Storage:** lockers are available to store carry-on bags whilst they enjoy the lounge space.

5. **Refresh:** lounges often have private showers. Imagine an end of day flight when your exec has been travelling from meeting to meeting in a hot environment. Getting on a 3 hour flight can make for an uncomfortable journey home, but factor in a shower at the lounge, and your exec is refreshed and ready to go.

6. **Recharge:** reclining chairs for short naps in private spaces. Some lounges have 'pods' for travellers to snooze in.

BA's Forty Winks Nap Lounge (Heathrow, UK, T5)

There are 2 types of lounges:

1. **Airline lounges:** the ones owned and managed by the airlines for their frequent flyers. For airline lounge access you need to be a frequent flyer, with the right level of points (with that airline or alliance) OR hold

a business class or first class ticket (with that alliance). If you are eligible to use an airline lounge, you do not have to pre-book to gain access.

2. **Airport lounges:** are separate. These are managed by groups such as Aspire, No.1 Lounges, Lounge Pass, Priority Pass, Executive Lounges etc. Airport lounges are available for **all** passengers to use, regardless of the airline they are flying with. Airport lounges are accessible by purchasing an access pass.

Using my previous CEO 'Alistair' as the example: he had silver frequent flyer status with BA. If Alistair was flying from London Heathrow to Cape Town with BA, he would be able to use the **Oneworld** lounge at Heathrow Airport. If he was flying with South African Airlines, he would use the **Star Alliance** lounge at Heathrow Airport (because South African Airlines is a Star Alliance member). If he was flying to Miami with Delta - he would be able to use the **Sky Team** lounge at Heathrow Airport (because Delta is part of the Sky Team alliance).

Airline lounges can be the epitome of luxury, offering spa treatments and fine dining for travellers, in a stylish and luxurious environment that looks and feels like a 5* hotel. They're geared for the frequent business traveller, they're tranquil, professional, and calm. Airline lounges provide an oasis for your executive to have some time out from the airport madness. To eat, drink, freshen up, and catch up with their emails, before taking that short or long-haul flight to their destination.

As discussed in the previous step, frequent flyer programmes can provide entrance to airline lounges, **but you must check entry criteria first**. Access depends on the number of miles or points your exec has accrued. Entry isn't guaranteed just because they hold a frequent flyer card, its permitted after a certain number of points or miles are obtained.

However, if your exec is flying business or first class, entry to the airline lounge will be included in their ticket price. But, for the economy traveller, you need to check eligibility through the frequent flyer membership portal (for the points total) and the lounge access policy (at that particular airport).

For 'airport' lounges, any passenger can gain access by purchasing a pass for one-off use, or you can purchase annual membership from a supplier, such as Priority Pass, which will get you access to multiple airport lounges for 1 year at a discounted rate.

Useful websites to check out are:

Loungebuddy.com	lounge information for all airports
Loungepass.com	similar
No1lounges.com	info on their own airport lounges
Executivelounges.com	info for Aspire lounges
Prioritypass.com	annual membership for airport lounges

If your exec isn't a member of a frequent flyer programme, but is taking a trip with a 2 hour wait time or longer, purchasing a pass to use at an airport lounge will make their business travel experience much more comfortable.

Some lounges offer single-entry passes, while others require lounge membership or frequent flyer programme membership. Prices for a single-entry lounge pass can range from £20 to £50. Membership fees range from £200 to £500 annually, but they include access to airport lounges worldwide.

Next time your exec is taking a flight, view the lounge options available at the departure airport. Can your exec access an airline lounge for free with their FF programme? If not, consider booking an airport lounge for a one-off fee. Explain the benefits to your exec before booking. Your exec will appreciate the level of detail you've shown, in your travel planning, and will be super grateful of the lounge pass and the productivity boost.

Add to Bible... Continue to build your Bible for every trip flown, by your executive. Add details of any lounges you book. Link the lounge booking page to your Bible, and keep a note of any login details.

 Every time your exec uses a lounge, ask them for their feedback afterwards. Was it comfortable? Did it allow them to be productive? Would they use it again? Most airports have multiple lounge options, so finding the right one for your exec could be by trial and error. If your exec didn't have a positive experience, try a different lounge next time.

Add to Bible... When your executive gives you feedback on a particular lounge, add it to your Bible document. Revisit your notes next time they fly that trip.

As you know, business trip planning is complex, and there are many elements involved in building a seamless itinerary for your exec. Executive Assistants often pick up the phone to book complex flights. You can't always check multi-city connections, or establish if a flight is refundable or transferable, just by using an online platform. Flights are expensive, so in order to clarify booking details, we pick up the phone and talk to a booking agent.

A call with a booking agent can either go relatively smoothly or frustratingly slowly, and the key to unlocking the quick efficient call with the agent, is clear communication.

In business travel – that means using **phonetics**. Sierra tango echo papa 15, will walk you through how to use the phonetic alphabet in more detail...

STEP 15. Alpha, Bravo, Charlie, Delta!

What comes after Delta?

Do you know your Phonetic Alphabet? Can you say the entire alphabet phonetically from A to Z, without referring to Google?

In the 1920s The International Telecommunication Union (ITU), produced the first phonetic alphabet. It was based on city names from around the world e.g. Amsterdam, Baltimore, Casablanca, Denmark, and so on.

The original phonetic alphabet was adjusted over time by the International Air Transport Association (IATA), and it was adopted by the North Atlantic Treaty Organization (NATO) in 1956.

Today, the NATO version is the globally established phonetic alphabet, and its used as standard, across the military services, the telecommunications sector (customer support centres), in aviation (pilots and air traffic control), the police, maritime (ships and coastguards), and other emergency services.

They all use the phonetic alphabet to spell out their communications clearly, to overcome any language barriers, and to avoid any errors.

The travel industry also adopted the use of the phonetic alphabet, to spell out reservation bookings, and flight codes. As an executive assistant, its good practice to use the phonetic code when communicating over the phone. It avoids a lot of confusion, minimises risk, and helps overcome any noisy background issues you might get when dealing with a call centre.

I first started using the phonetic alphabet whilst in the EA to the CEO UK role, at Teleperformance. As a direct consequence of booking so many flights, I was constantly talking to booking agents, from the travel management company 'Egencia'.

There were occasional misunderstandings, when I gave a flight booking confirmation number to an agent during a call. I'm talking about the travel booking reference that looks like: C5CEKV or GKLDMC or 3JYGFR, you get the picture. If I was misheard, it meant I had to repeat the code to the booking agent again, and this delayed the booking agent in accessing the flight reservation I wanted to discuss urgently.

My solution to this problem was to do what the experts do and use the phonetic alphabet, when spelling out the flight confirmation code. Once I learnt it, I found that I started using it in a number of different situations to spell out key information.

Amending flight reservations, spelling surnames, giving pick up addresses and postcodes can all be done more effectively when using the phonetic alphabet. It's also useful when providing your executive's name to private driver companies for nameboards, and communicating the flight number.

I realised quite quickly, that this newly adopted skill was really very handy. It's also fun to see how quick you can become at using it, and your colleagues will be impressed listening to you in the office! I use this skill every day. It's definitely improved my communications when using the phone, it speeds up conversations, and minimises any confusion when imparting information or spelling passenger names.

Take a look at the phonetic alphabet on the next page. Try spelling your bosses surname out loud, or the street address for your office, or a recent flight booking code. Then try saying them out loud without looking at the page. Learning and using the phonetics alphabet, will transform a lot of booking conversations you have, and it's fun to use. Try it!

The Phonetic Alphabet

A	Alfa		**N**	November
B	Bravo		**O**	Oscar
C	Charlie		**P**	Papa
D	Delta		**Q**	Quebec
E	Echo		**R**	Romeo
F	Foxtrot		**S**	Sierra
G	Golf		**T**	Tango
H	Hotel		**U**	Uniform
I	India		**V**	Victor
J	Juliett		**W**	Whiskey
K	Kilo		**X**	X-Ray
L	Lima		**Y**	Yankee
M	Mike		**Z**	Zulu

Miscommunication is a waste of time, and can be completely frustrating. It's especially problematic if you're trying to move a flight booking at short notice. The clock's ticking, and you're falling over at the first hurdle, which is getting the agent to understand which flight you're talking about. Using the phonetic alphabet will eradicate this issue. If you use the phonetic alphabet to spell out your booking code, you'll communicate clearly the first time around and get straight into the detail.

Using the phonetic alphabet when speaking on the phone, can help ensure clear and accurate communication, especially when dealing with names, addresses, or any information that involves spelling out words, or using letters and numbers.

Have a copy of the phonetic alphabet handy, whether it's a printed chart, or a capture on your desktop. When you need to communicate a letter, use the corresponding word from the phonetic alphabet. For example, instead of saying "B," say "Bravo." For a booking confirmation code C5CEKV say Charlie 5 Charlie Echo Kilo Victor.

Practice using the phonetic alphabet every day. It should become second nature to you. Next time you're making yourself a hot drink, say the name of your coffee brand out loud, or your brand of tea bags, using phonetics. Practice saying the days of the week, your bosses full name or your company address.

Don't just use it for business purposes, use it for personal administration. An insurance quote, a policy number, a reference number, your postcode. You'll be surprised how you ever managed without it!

STEP 16. The Hub Airport

Building your knowledge of your exec's business travel preferences, is essential to providing 'next level' executive assistant support. In Step 9, you established your exec's top 3 hotels, in the locations they travel to the most. Next, it's time to focus on their air travel, and if your supporting a senior leader, heading to the airport will be part of their weekly routine.

Completing 'due diligence' on the airports available to your exec, when travelling from their home address, is vital. Travelling from home to a destination is the 'outbound' part of the trip, and your exec could live in an area with more than one outbound airport to choose from.

Every airport is different in terms of its destination options, airline providers, daily routes, timetables, and connecting flights. There are small regional airports, and there a large international airports.

Your exec may live close by to a regional airport, but that airport may be limited in its flight options. **Regional airports** often focus on seasonal or holiday destinations, and provide infrequent domestic flights. Whilst the larger **international airports** are going to offer frequent daily flights with earlier flight times, to global city destinations, which accommodate the business traveller.

International airports are known as **hubs** because of their greater connectivity for airlines and passengers. **Your executive's hub airport is the airport closest to their home address, with the most flight options available, for business travellers.**

In 2021-2022 I supported 'Jürgen', the CTO of the EMEA and APAC regions of a US tech company called Ciena. Jürgen lived in Austria, his closest airport was 'Linz' (LNZ) and Linz was only 15 mins drive away from Jürgen's home address. For the newbie EA in the role (i.e. myself) Linz Airport seemed like an excellent choice for Jürgen's business travel.

Airport transfers would be quick because of the proximity of his home address to LNZ airport. "How many C-level execs have an airport only 15 mins drive away?" I wondered. Coordinating his business travel is going to be a cinch, I thought to myself. Unfortunately, I was wrong.

Linz (which almost sounds like a well-known chocolate confectioner) proved to be a bit of a chocolate teapot. It closed down during the pandemic, and was very slow to re-open. It had maybe 3 outbound flights a day (on a good day) and it was just pootling along, not doing a lot, or providing much of a service.

Of course, Linz's website confidently boasts that the airport is "The gateway to the World!", and I really wished that were true when I was in that EA role.

Even the domestic flights out of Linz, connecting to other airports, were useless. They only seemed to operate twice a week, and then that was mid-morning which was of no use to me or my boss. Business travellers are early birds, they want early flights to get them to their destination at the start of the business day, not by mid-afternoon. Naturally, I discounted Linz quite quickly from my business travel planning, and I soon discovered that my manager's hub airport was going to be Vienna.

Vienna or VIE was further for my exec to travel to, from his home address (2 hours). But it provided the flight routes I was looking for (international) and the frequency. Vienna catered for the business traveller, it had direct early morning flights to multiple European destinations, plus it offered direct, indirect and connecting flights to the US, Canada, and Dubai.

Where's your executive's **hub airport**? Ask your exec if they only have 1 outbound airport option, or is there another you should consider, when trip planning. Your exec may have a preferred airport, depending on whether they're flying domestic or international. If you don't ask them, you could be missing out on vital information. Your exec has local knowledge on the area they live in - you don't.

Add to Bible...

With the hub airport confirmed, add it to your Bible. If you book travel for more than 1 exec, ask each one about their local airport, and their hub airport. Add all the info to your Bible.

Now that you've identified your executive's hub airport (for their outbound flight), it's time to consider the airport closest to your office. Which is the hub airport for your office location? Where do visiting executives fly into, when travelling to your office?

If you work in central London, this is likely to be either London Heathrow (LHR) or London Gatwick (LGW). Let's say LGW is the most conveniently located to your office. When was the last time you personally visited LGW? Yes, YOU. Not your exec, you, as booker.

As the travel booker, its crucial you're familiar with the international airport that's closest to your office. This will be your office 'hub' airport.

Building your knowledge on the 'office' airport, is useful on many levels:

1. **Point of Contact:** you maybe the point of contact at your office, for other visiting execs and their EAs. In which case you need the answers to their questions on business travel.
2. **External Visitors:** if a visitor is meeting with your exec, and is travelling to the meeting from another country or state, you can support them with travel advice.
3. **Transfers:** knowing the transfer routes, timings, and options, will help you to help others.
4. **Flights:** your exec may or may not, live close by to your office, but there will be times when your exec will use this airport. This is the 2nd hub airport you should research.

I strongly recommend you complete an in-person familiarisation trip, to your office's hub airport (if possible). You can gain a wealth of information from an airport's website, but nothing will match the experience of travelling to that airport, standing in the check-in area, and understanding how business executives travel through the terminal, to catch their flight.

By attending in-person and viewing the office's hub airport, you'll vastly increase your knowledge as the travel booker, and improve your expertise at building travel itineraries. You'll discover airport facilities which you didn't know existed, and you'll appreciate the scale of the terminal building.

You'll also have a better understanding of the parking facilities available, the transport links to different terminals, and the location of the airport lounges and onsite restaurants. There may be an airport shuttle service you weren't aware of, which could shave minutes off your travel planning.

Plan a visit to your office's airport. Request a tour from the airport's marketing team, and explain that you're a frequent business travel booker and would benefit from a show around. If there are several EAs at your office which are co-ordinating business travel from the same airport, see if you can organise a group visit and a pre-arranged airport tour.

When you're at the airport, familiarise yourself with the airport layout, the distance between check-in and the departure gates. View the parking services available (valet parking) and the transportation links. Where's the private driver drop off area? Where's the meet and greet area? Picture your exec moving through the airport. What more can you do to support them, and to enhance their business travel experience?

Visiting your hub airport will help you with travel timings in future, as you've experienced the layout first-hand.

View the **Airport Familiarisation Checklist** on the next page. Take it with you when you go. Tick off the items on the list as you walk around, to ensure you've gathered as much information as possible, from your in-person tour. Take notes and add to your Bible on your return.

If it isn't possible for a group of EAs from your company, to complete an airport familiarisation trip in-person, invite the airport to come to you! Approach their marketing or communications team, ask if they could host a webinar for your company's EAs (the travel bookers), to demonstrate the facilities available at the airport, and to provide a Q&A session.

Airport Familiarisation Checklist

(For use when visiting your Office's Hub Airport)

Ground Transportation
- [ ] Where can private drivers drop off/pick up passengers
- [ ] Where can private drivers 'meet & greet' travellers on arrival
- [ ] Is there a dedicated taxi company at the airport and where
- [ ] Train: the overland connections to/from airport, which terminal
- [ ] Underground/metro: connections to/from airport, which terminal
- [ ] City airport bus: to/from which terminal
- [ ] Car parking: what is available e.g. short stay, long stay, pre-booking, online reservations, valet parking, fees
- [ ] Travel from car park to terminal (shuttle bus/pod) journey time
- [ ] Hotel shuttle services available

The Airport
- [ ] Airport hotels available (if required night before flight)
- [ ] Number of terminals, terminal maps
  - o Airlines operating at each terminal
  - o Travel options between terminals (monorail, shuttle bus, walk, and time taken for each)
- [ ] Check-in options
  - o Fast track security
  - o Bag drop area
  - o Self-service check-in
- [ ] Lounges
  - o Lounges available at airport
  - o Compatibility with your exec's airline alliance
  - o Access fees
  - o Terminal locations
  - o Showers, sleep pods
- [ ] Amenities for the business traveller
  - o Meeting rooms, quiet zones, fitness centre
  - o Wi-Fi access
- [ ] What's the IATA airport code

Airport Communications
- [ ] E-newsletter, Twitter, Facebook, Airport App
- [ ] Airport loyalty programme (Heathrow Rewards)
- [ ] Business traveller forum

Establish a personal relationship with the airport's marketing or communications team. Is there a forum you could join, to give feedback to on behalf of the business travellers within your company? Become your company's representative for business travellers, at your hub airport.

If it's impossible to visit your office's hub airport in-person, because it's too far to travel to (or if your remote), and if the airport won't commit to a webinar for travel bookers, the next best thing is YouTube.

Search YouTube for videos of the airport, and watch those recorded by genuine travellers. You don't want the glossy PR videos; you want real traveller videos that alert you to any problems or additional facilities that you weren't aware of.

You're making great progress in your steps to implementing executive assistant mastery. Researching hub airports is time consuming, but it's a worthwhile exercise. No doubt you've uncovered lots of information about your hub airport, that you weren't aware of.

When you've updated your Bible with the essential information, move on to Step 17. Airport Transfers.

STEP 17. Airport Transfers

How does your exec travel to their hub airport from home? With their hub airport established, it's time to take a look at how they actually get there.

In my experience, some EAs and admins only book flights and hotels, they drop them into their exec's calendar and consider that to be 'job done'. They don't book airport transfers. The exec can sort out their own travel to the airport because they know the route, they can call a cab, right? Wrong.

Without any pre-booked transfers in place, the exec is left to sort out their own transport to the airport, on top of everything else they need to focus upon. It's 'another thing to do' for the exec, and its adding to the list of things that could go disastrously wrong before the flight departure.

Letting your exec book their own transfers is simply bad practice. It doesn't demonstrate a duty of care to the travelling exec, and it certainly doesn't show them 'next level' EA support. I don't subscribe to that level of service; I offer my travellers what I call the 'VIP' travel service. I co-ordinate their travel from the moment they leave their home address, to the moment they reach their destination, and everything in between. Skipping the step of organising airport transfers is a 'no go' in my opinion. Why wouldn't you do this for your exec? You're their executive assistant.

When your exec leaves their 'home' address for a business trip, that's the beginning of their journey (not the airport). Getting your exec to the airport on time to catch their flight is critical, so why leave it to chance? EAs have time to plan this step, to research the route, to check the transport timings, and to pre-book and pre-pay. Your executive doesn't have the time, and it's not their job either.

Trip planning should start from the business traveller's home address, and end with the business traveller's home address, and everything in between. By pre booking the airport transfers, you're reducing the risk of them arriving late at the airport, and that could have disastrous consequences.

There are multiple ways for your exec to travel from home to the airport, to catch their flight. It depends on their country and region, but the usual options are:

1. Self-drive (using their own car)
2. Taxi, Cab, Uber
3. Executive car / private driver
4. Train

When I supported the CTO who was based in Austria, he lived so far away from a hub airport (2 hours journey time) that his best type of transfer was rail. However, the majority of senior execs I've supported, live within 30 mins of a major airport hub, and this is when your options for airport transfers really open up.

Schedule time with your exec to ask specifically about their usual route to the airport. Self-drive, taxi, uber, private driver, train etc. Ask them what's working now, and what hasn't worked previously (so you know which options have been explored already). Confirm their full address details (for driver pickups), and the average time it takes for them to travel to the airport.

Whatever mode of transport your exec prefers, to get to the airport, always work with them to get it pre-booked and in the calendar. Airport transfers are an essential component of travel logistics, as they get your exec to the airport terminal on time.

When your exec has landed at their destination airport, the airport transfer is the next element of their journey. Either from airport arrivals to their hotel, or airport arrivals to the meeting room location or the office.

Airport transfers 'wrap around' each flight, and well planned transfers will make your exec's travel experience feel smooth and effortless. During 1 business trip, you'll be planning (and booking) a total of 4 transfers:

Outbound:

    (1) Home to airport departures

    (2) Airport arrivals to hotel, meeting location or office

Inbound:

    (3) Hotel, meeting location, or office to airport departures

    (4) Airport arrivals to home.

For the outbound transfer, your exec is the best person to ask what works because they've completed this trip many times. They know the length of the journey, the time to allow, and they'll know if this changes during peak or off-peak times. Add all of this information to your Bible.

 Add to Bible... If you're supporting multiple execs with their travel, ask each one for their airport transfer preferences. Build your traveller profiles for each person. If they have their own preferred driver service, ask for a name, contact details and how they pay for the service. Can you pre-pay for them or do they pay via cash or card, in the car?

For the short hops (airport transfers of 5-15 mins journey time) any pre-booked car service is usually fine. You'll know from speaking to your exec, which taxi or cab company they favour, or if they use Uber.

For the longer journeys (15-30 mins journey time) I suggest you book an executive car service (also known as a private driver) because it gives your exec a better travel experience, and they can be more productive during the transfer. *Step 18 is devoted to executive cars and private drivers.*

If your exec travels to the airport by train, ask for their preferred departure and arrival stations. Record all the information in your Bible, so you can refer to this next time your planning their business travel.

Finally, if your exec communicates to you that they sort out their transfers themselves, **encourage them to let you manage the process**. Afterall, it's your responsibility, to get them to the airport on time.

I once supported a CEO, 'Anders', who travelled to CPH airport on a weekly basis. He lived 30 minutes' drive away from the airport, and was using a private hire taxi company. I was new to the role, and during the handover with my predecessor, she advised me that Anders booked his own transfers. "You don't have to worry about it," she confirmed.

After 1 week in the role, I had a 1:1 with Anders. I asked him why he was managing his own transfers. "Because I've always done it," he said.
"Can I manage your transfers for you, from now on?" I asked him.
"Yes please!" he replied. "That's one less thing for me to think about!"

 Save your executive's time, by managing airport transfers for them. Plan the transfers, pre-book the transfers, and manage the payment. Your exec simply hops in the vehicle, travels stress free, and pops out the other end. Job done.

STEP 18. Executive Cars & Private Drivers

When I first supported 'Alistair', the CEO of Teleperformance UK, I asked him about his airport transfer preferences. He explained that he lived outside of central London, and relatively close to London Heathrow Airport. In fact 'LHR' was a maximum 30 minutes' drive away, from his home address.

Alistair explained he used a private driver to pick him up, and drop him off, at the terminal building. A small independent executive car service was already in place, and he'd been using it for some time. Alistair confirmed he was happy with the level of service he'd been receiving from 'Neil'.

Neil was a small independent business owner who had one executive car, which he drove himself. He'd been providing Alistair with his airport transfers for a number of years. 'Fantastic!' I thought. I don't have to do anything here. The service provider is in place, and it's all working well.

I asked for Neil's contact details, and gave him a call. I introduced myself as Alistair's new EA, and asked how he'd like to receive booking requests in future, and what information he required. I also asked if he charged for 'wait time', was there a fixed price for airport transfers, if he provided a 'meet and greet' service, and how he tracked inbound flights (so I wouldn't have to communicate any flight delays to him).

Neil gave me clear instructions on what he needed, and his preferred booking method was via email. He confirmed that he tracked flights from his mobile, and that I didn't need to communicate any flight delays to him for the inbound flights. He said he provided a meet and greet service, and he'd wait in arrivals for Alistair. Marvellous! I could tell that Neil and I, were going to work well together.

For the home pick-ups (the outbounds) Neil confirmed he needed the pick-up time at Alistair's home address, and the terminal number for the drop-off.

For the airport pick-ups (the inbounds) Neil confirmed he required the terminal number, flight number, and the departure time, emailed over to him (so he could track the flight), and he'd confirm the booking by return email.

I'm so pleased that I had that initial conversation with Neil, because it really helped to establish our working relationship. He was a small business owner, and we worked together for a number of years supporting Alistair, who was a regular business traveller.

The home to airport transfers (and returns) always operated smoothly, and it was reassuring to have the continuity of service, and professional support, from Neil, when I was booking business travel for my CEO.

There are many benefits of using a **private driver** (as we refer to them in the UK). You may be familiar with the term 'private driver' or 'chauffeur' dependent on the country you live in, and they generally amount to the same thing. However, there is a big difference between private hire taxis, cabs, and ubers, versus **executive cars**.

Taxis, cabs, and ubers, provide a great service, but the cars are pretty standard, and the level of service delivered can vary, depending on the driver you're allocated. This means that you could be lucky and get great service, or you could get a dirty car, with a rude or scruffy driver who is late, and blames the traffic.

Business travel is an important element of our responsibility, and so much can go wrong if it isn't planned effectively. Why would you leave an airport transfer to chance, by booking a taxi company you're unfamiliar with?

Alternatively, you could spend a few minutes more on planning and research, enabling you to book an executive car service in advance, that's 100% reliable. An executive car arrives on time, collects your business traveller on time, and most importantly, gets them to the airport on time.

An executive car service is far superior to the service provided by taxis, cabs, and ubers, and as EAs we strive to supply a higher level of service, to our business travellers. There are so many benefits of booking a private driver or chauffeur, via an executive car service, particularly for airport transfers.

| 4G WiFi Onboard | Bottled Water | Daily Newspaper | Child Seats Available | Free Meet + Greet |

Let's take a deeper dive into the benefits of using an executive car service, for your business traveller.

14 x Benefits of using an Executive Car Service

1. **Peace of mind:** eliminate any potential travel risks, delays, or no-shows by booking in advance.
2. **Timing:** once you've shared the route and desired drop-off time, the supplier will often guide you on the exact pick-up time.
3. **Fixed price:** suppliers will charge a fixed price (agreed at the time of booking) and any 'wait time' is included, together with any fees they incur for parking, waiting, or access to the drop-off zone.
4. **Ease of booking:** larger suppliers provide online booking platforms, making regular bookings easier to navigate, track and expense.
5. **Notifications:** your traveller will receive a text message when the driver is outside, together with the driver's name, vehicle registration and exact location.
6. **Flight monitoring:** they'll monitor the flight arrival time, and wait for your traveller if the flight's delayed.
7. **Airport 'meet and greet' service:** the driver will wait in arrivals with a nameboard. This is incredibly useful, and I've used this service hundreds of times. It's a quick 'connect' between driver and passenger, and provides a seamless transition from the airport to the executive car.
8. **Luggage:** drivers help with luggage, without being asked. They don't grumble either.
9. **Business class experience:** drivers are smart and courteous, often wearing a suit or shirt and tie. The car interior is immaculate, and so is the exterior. Your boss travels like a VIP.
10. **Device connectivity:** cars have Wi-Fi onboard and charging points.
11. **Comfort:** often equipped with bottled water, daily newspaper, and air con.
12. **Focus time:** executive car drivers know when to talk, and when not to. Your exec won't have to make 'small talk' for the duration of the journey, which means they can focus on their email or make a call.
13. **Luxury vehicle:** a luxury car gives the passenger more room to use their laptop, or make a call in a quiet environment, with passenger privacy. The

bigger the supplier, the more vehicle options will be available to you when booking.

14. **Safety**: a reputable supplier will vet their drivers carefully. Only the drivers that have passed various security and reference checks, will make the grade.

 In Step 17 you discovered how your exec travels to the airport. If your exec already has a private driver in place (like Alistair), reach out to the supplier direct. Make a connection. Talk to them, and familiarise yourself with the services they provide. Who drives your boss? What's the booking process? How do you make payment?

 Does the supplier your exec already uses, offer a 'meet and greet' service? What else can you do to improve their transfers? Are there any other services you don't know about? The supplier might have improved their technology with SMS driver updates, which you haven't signed up for yet.

 Maybe your exec doesn't use an executive car service for home pick-ups, or hasn't found the right supplier. Finding the right supplier can take time, so don't give up at the first hurdle. Shortlist three suppliers and trial each one. Advise your exec you're going to put three suppliers through their paces, over the next three airport runs. Ask your exec for feedback on each one. Consider the easiness of booking each supplier, was it quick, efficient, and professional?

 Add to Bible... Update your Bible with the supplier's information. Add the date when you put the supplier in place, and the services they provide (meet and greet, text updates, maximum wait time). Add any fixed price details, if known.

 If you've put a new supplier in place, add an entry to your calendar called 'driver feedback' for 1 months' time. When the time comes, ask your exec if they are still happy with the executive car service. It's essential to have regular check-ins with your boss on their performance. Share any feedback directly with the supplier.

Ultimately, a supplier wants to keep your business, so let them know if things aren't working as well as they should be. If you experience a bad provider for a particular trip, add that in your Bible too, so you know not to use them again in future.

One thing I should caveat about using an executive car service, is that it's going to be **off policy** with your corporate travel programme. In other words, it's 'off limits' for your standard business traveller. Your corporate travel programme will allow taxis, cabs and uber, but it probably won't even mention executive car hire. But don't let this deceive you. Corporate travel managers are fully aware that senior level executives use this service, it's just 'off the radar' for the standard employee.

This is largely due to costs, as a taxi, cab, or uber is a perfectly adequate means of transport for most travellers, and will be less expensive than an executive car. But for the senior level execs (the C-level and the SVPs of your business), there will be hidden options.

To discover what's really available for senior execs within your business, ask the most senior EAs in your country or region. Afterall, booking private drivers and executive cars isn't about travelling in luxury, or being treated like a VIP. It's about enabling your exec to work effectively whilst in transit, improving their productivity, and delivering them to the airport or office on time.

During my career, I've worked for three different companies who had in-house private drivers. Yes, direct employees who drove executive cars for the company. Not just in London, but nationwide. This was an 'elite' support service that operated in several locations across the UK. Their existence wasn't communicated in the travel policy, or company handbook. The service was very much 'offline'. The only way I found out about it, was from a board level EA within the company.

 If your employed by a large multinational corporation, and you exec travels internationally to offices owned by your company, contact your 'go to person' at that location for local knowledge. Ask them for their private driver recommendations. It's likely that an EA at that destination will have a supplier they can share with you, and they may already have a corporate account in place.

 If your boss is travelling to an unfamiliar city location, that isn't associated with a company site, you won't have a private driver on speed dial. Instead of searching on Google to find a reputable local supplier (which is never guaranteed, and I speak from experience), one solution is to contact the hotel where your exec will be staying, and ask them.

My timesaving tip is to contact 'Concierge' at your exec's hotel and ask them direct. Concierge services will either recommend an executive car service they know, or will offer to book it for you. They know who to use and who to avoid, so don't waste time on independent research.

STEP 19. Frequent Travel Dashboard

Is your boss a frequent traveller, a road warrior, or an EMEA or APAC corporate executive? If you work for a large multinational that has multiple offices across the globe, it's guaranteed that your boss will fly to in-person meetings, site visits, and industry events, on a regular basis. The flights could be domestic, international, or a combination of both.

Over a period of time, you'll recognise that your exec is flying repeat trips. They'll travel to the same sites and locations, time after time. Whether its weekly, monthly, every few weeks, or quarterly.

View the example below, of a business traveller's proposed schedule, for the next 7 weeks. Notice the repeat trips, and the number of hotel nights required.

> Week 1: LHR to JFK, stay 3 nights and return.
> Week 2: LHR to CPT, stay 4 nights and return.
> Week 3: LHR to CDG, stay 2 nights and return.
> Week 4: Work from home / Bristol office.
> Week 5: LHR to JFK, 3 nights, return.
> Week 6: LHR to CDG, 2 nights, return.
> Week 7: LHR to CPT, 4 nights, return.

The repeat business travel itineraries, you build for your own executive, will form a pattern. For each frequently flown trip, they'll fly the same route, with the same airline, and stay at the same hotel (availability permitting). So, when you've hit on a winning travel itinerary for that particular destination, you repeat it.

If a particular preferred hotel isn't available, you'll have to book a different one, but the route flown, and the airline operator, will generally be the same, every time your exec visits a particular location.

Every time you co-ordinate travel, to the same destination, you're basically replicating the last trip, and you should capture all the elements of the trip planning in your Bible, for future use. Your Bible should also include how to schedule meetings at that site, who to contact at that location, and any other information that's helpful when co-ordinating your executive's time at the destination.

However, there's another resource I've developed, which I've found immensely useful. It's a 1 pager, a 'cheat sheet', which captures the bare bones of each trip. It's my quick reference guide, and I refer to it whenever a trip has been confirmed, and I need to source flights and accommodation at lightning speed.

I call this 1 pager the **frequent travel dashboard.** It's organised by city, and only includes the locations my exec travels to regularly. It shows the trip duration, the routes flown, the flight operators, and the preferred hotels.

The frequent travel dashboard gives me the facts at a glance, and I use it when I'm pricing a new trip. As soon as I've got the confirmed dates of travel, I visit my dashboard, which gives me the data I need. It's my 'go to' resource when I get the green light to co-ordinate a new trip.

 Repeat business trips often form the same patterns, so its beneficial to document the logistics of each trip, so you can refer to it next time around.

View the frequent travel dashboard on the next page. It shows the frequently travelled routes, for a UK CEO, who uses London Heathrow as their outbound airport. It lists the cities he visits, the specific area of the city, and the likely duration of the trip. It displays the mode of transport e.g. flight or train, the preferred air carriers who fly that route, and the outbound and inbound airports by their IATA codes. It also includes the preferred hotels at each destination.

FREQUENT TRAVEL DASHBOARD
for CEO UK

NEW YORK

Area: Downtown Manhattan
Trip Duration: 4 days
Transport: Flight
Operator: British Airways, Virgin Atlantic
Route: LHR-JFK or LGA
Preferred Hotel: Westin Times Square, Marriott Marquis

MIAMI

Area: Miami Beach
Trip Duration: 5 days
Transport: Flight
Operator: British Airways, Virgin Atlantic, American Airlines
Route: LHR-MIA
Preferred Hotel: Loews Miami Beach, Royal Palm

CAPE TOWN

Area: City Centre
Trip Duration: 5 days
Transport: Flight
Operator: British Airways, Virgin Atlantic
Route: LHR-CPT
Preferred Hotels: Table Bay, Hilton, Victoria & Alfred

NEW DELHI

Area: Gurgaon
Trip Duration: 4 days
Transport: Flight
Operator: British Airways, Air India, Virgin Atlantic
Route: LHR-DEL
Preferred Hotel: The Oberoi, The Westin, Trident

LONDON

Area: Square Mile
Trip Duration: 2 days
Transport: Train
Operator: Southwest Trains
Route: n/a
Preferred Hotel: Leonards Royal St Pauls, Mercure London Bridge

GLASGOW

Area: City Centre
Trip Duration: 2 days
Transport: Flight
Operator: British Airways
Route: LHR-GLA
Preferred Hotel: Blythswood Square, Marriott City Centre

If you're new to your EA post, you'll receive handover training from your predecessor, and business travel will be one of the areas covered. But if handover hasn't been an option, it's imperative you understand your exec's frequently flown trips, because these are the trips you'll be co-ordinating regularly.

Building a **frequent travel dashboard** is a productivity hack you'll benefit from using, whether your new or well established in your role. It's about mapping a process, identifying the frequent trips your boss flies, and documenting them.

A frequent travel dashboard acts as a 1 page 'cheat sheet' to refer to, every time your tasked with costing, and building, a repeat business trip for your boss. You won't need to ask your boss about the route flown, or destination airport, just visit the dashboard.

Booking business travel can be a time consuming process, but if you can document the frequently flown routes, you can refer back to your notes next time they make that trip. This saves you time when co-ordinating a repeat trip because you've already captured the previous route flown, the airline carrier you used, the hotel provider you booked, and the number of hotel nights your exec required.

The frequent travel dashboard will become your **quick reference guide**, for future trip costing and planning. You can continue to build your **frequent travel dashboard**, as and when you recognise a repeat trip. You should build separate dashboards for each exec you support.

To build your frequent travel dashboard, visit the information already held in your Bible, plus previous entries in your exec's calendar. You can also view booking histories via your online travel platform (your TMC).

Build a frequent travel dashboard for each executive you support. You'll have their business travel logistics at your fingertips. Next time you're asked to book business travel, you won't have to search the calendar for the previous trip details, just visit your travel dashboard, your 'cheat sheet', for the data.

Add to Bible...

As well as saving your dashboard to your desktop, snip it and drop it into your Bible. Your Bible is always your number one resource, your master document, so keep a copy of it towards the front, before the breakdown of information for each office, or operational, site your exec visits.

STEP 20. Travel Planning Checklist

Back in January 2012, I started a new job as Executive Assistant to the CEO UK, at Teleperformance. It's one of those companies that's massive, but nobody's ever heard of. When I joined, there were 400,000 employees globally, with 10,000 employees in the UK. Teleperformance manages customer services, for businesses who outsource that element of their business operation. You may be more familiar with the alternative terms for customer service, such as 'customer experience' or 'CX'.

Teleperformance has teams of customer service agents, all around the world. Supporting global brands and managing their customer enquiries via online chat, voice, and email. You've probably had a direct communication with one of their agents in the past 48 hours, you just weren't aware you were talking to an agent employed by Teleperformance. Lots of companies outsource their CX operations to Teleperformance, and they work on behalf of numerous well-known brands, across multiple sectors.

When I joined in 2012, I had direct and relevant experience with another outsourcing provider called 'Integreon', but it was nowhere near the scale of Teleperformance, or 'TP UK' (as we called it in-house). At Integreon, I'd been supporting the EVP of business development. Integreon had 1,000 employees total, and the EVP travelled internationally, albeit infrequently.

So, joining TP UK was like a baptism of fire. I'd gone from a company with 1,000 employees in total, to one with 10,000 in just one region. I thought I'd worked for a fast paced company, but I didn't know there was another level, until I joined TP UK.

My new boss 'Alistair' was the CEO of the UK, Ireland, and South Africa, and he was also new to the business. He joined a few weeks before I did. Being new to the business, he was keen to view the entire UK, Ireland, and South Africa operations for himself, and that meant visiting our largest sites on a regular basis.

Alistair was responsible for a total of 27 sites across the UK, Ireland, and South Africa. Our UK headquarters were in Bristol, where I lived at the time. Alistair lived in the Southeast, with 30 mins travel time, to London Heathrow Airport.

My first week in the role at TP UK had been spent onboarding, and completing handover, and my second week was when I was thrown-in at the deep end. I realised then, that the handover I'd received hadn't really scratched the surface, as it had focussed on systems and people, rather than locations and travel routes. But you can't expect everything in a handover, and I was fortunate enough to have received some introductions, and system training, from my predecessor.

But what I really wanted was access to a digital file, listing all of our sites across the UK, South Africa, and Ireland (the region my CEO was responsible for). Together with the site addresses, nearby hotels, key contacts at each site, and airport transfer times. Unfortunately, I didn't find such a file because it didn't exist, and the information wasn't on the company intranet, or the shared directory. I had to start from scratch, and gather the information, for all of the 27 sites.

It took me several weeks to build my knowledge, and my **Bible** document for TP UK. To date, it's the largest Bible document I've ever owned, at 148 pages long (A4 size). The importance of building an executive assistant Bible, and how to build one, is covered in Step 3. It's a critical step, and once it's built it saves you so much time with trip planning, scheduling meetings at other sites, and a whole host of other tasks. It's a total life saver.

When I'd got my TP UK Bible into a reasonable shape (and at that point it was nowhere near 148 pages, more like 30), the next process I wanted to improve was business travel co-ordination.

At TP UK, I was always knee deep in travel planning, and I once commented to a colleague who sat next to me, "I feel like a hamster on a wheel", because of the speed I was working at, just to keep up. Alistair was averaging 2-4 flights a week, every week, so you can imagine the amount of time I was spending on travel co-ordination.

I felt anxious about the number of flights, hotels, and transfers, I was pricing and booking in quick succession. It didn't feel normal. In the CX sector there is a term 'ramp up', that refers to increasing resources (agents), in order to meet high demands of customer enquiries, following a campaign launch or product promotion. I thought that due to the high demand of travel requests I was receiving, I needed to find a way to 'ramp up' myself.

As I was fully responsible for co-ordinating the CEO's business travel, with no access to additional support, I knew I needed to work smarter. I wanted a process, or system, to help me to become faster when booking travel, and co-ordinating trips, but I couldn't skip on the detail. What I required was a 'checklist'.

My solution was to create a **travel planning checklist** that I could refer to, whenever I was booking the flights, hotel, and transfers, for each trip. Because of the speed I had to work at, and the complexity of the travel bookings, I was convinced that a checklist would guide me, to complete the booking and scheduling, quickly, accurately, and flawlessly. Plus, I also had the CFO to look after, another frequent business traveller.

The trips I co-ordinated for Alistair, were a mix of UK domestic and international. He was a weekly business traveller, a road warrior. A UK week would usually consist of two to three UK destinations. He would fly Glasgow and back in one day, Belfast in a day, and Newcastle would also be a same day return. An international trip would be travel to Miami, Cairo, Cape Town, or another global Teleperformance location.

I estimate that during my five years at TP UK, supporting Alistair, I co-ordinated 1,500 domestic and international trips. The **travel planning checklist** that I built, whilst at TP UK, has served me extremely well. It's been updated as I've changed employers, but the content of that checklist is largely the same. It's a checklist that I've used multiple times a week, for each trip I'm working on, and at TP UK I was working on an average of 6 trips at a time.

My trusty travel planning checklist prompts me, to consider all elements of the booking process. It helps me to deliver what I call the 'VIP traveller' service. I plan everything, from the moment my traveller leaves their home address, to the moment they arrive at their destination, and everything in between. I plan their ground transfers, arrival at the terminal building, fast track security, their inflight seat preference (aisle or window), extra legroom, and the class of travel allowed in-line with company policy.

The checklist reminds me, to ensure that the traveller's frequent flyer number, has been attached to their flight booking. That their hotel preferences are adopted, and to attach their hotel loyalty membership number, where possible.

As well as helping me through the booking process, the travel planning checklist prompts me to add the travel bookings and logistics to my exec's calendar. It alerts me to add the transfers, check-ins, and flights, into the calendar in the right order, so I don't miss anything out.

The traveller's calendar must accurately reflect everything I'm booking, and guide the traveller through the travel process at the right time. **The calendar is the digital itinerary**, which is why it must capture every single trip detail, for my business traveller. View the checklist on the next page, see how much detail there is to think about when trip planning.

✈ TRAVEL PLANNING CHECKLIST

AIRPORT OUT: **DESTINATION:**   **DATE:**

AIRPORT IN: **DESTINATION:**   **DATE:**

CALENDAR
Add city destination top and time zone
Show time zone left hand side

COUNTRY ENTRY
Covid entry requirements
Visa entry requirements
Local weather

FLIGHT RESERVATION
Economy / Premium / Business
Attach Frequent flyer number
Hold baggage
Carry-on baggage
Priority boarding
Extra leg room
Seat preference (aisle / window)
Seat no. outbound
Seat no. inbound
Fast track security pass outbound
Fast track security pass inbound
Lounge access

ACCOMMODATION RESERVATION
King size bed
Corporate rate
Loyalty scheme
Concierge for Transfer service

GROUND TRANSFERS

Outbound
Terminal no.
1. Home to Airport departures
(driver/self-drive/train/parking)
2. Airport arrival to office or hotel
(train / shuttle / taxi / self-drive)
Meet and greet with name board if driver

Inbound
Terminal no.
3. Hotel or Office to Departure airport
(train / shuttle / taxi)
4. Airport arrivals to home
Meet and greet with name board if driver

☐ TRIP COMPLETED

MEETINGS
Meetings confirmed / local teams
Addresses of all meetings / sites
Agenda / supporting documents / lunch

FACILITIES
Meeting rooms / catering / dinners
Desk booking / security / entry to building

ADD TO CALENDAR

Flight outbound		Flight Inbound
☐	Time zone	☐
☐	Block flight time / add flight ref no.	☐
☐	24 hour clock	☐
☐	Arrival time	☐
☐	Carrier	☐
☐	Terminal out / terminal inbound	☐
☐	Seat no.	☐
☐	Baggage allowance	☐
☐	Full booking details to calendar	☐
☐	PDF of booking attached	☐
☐	Airport check-in (full booking and pdf)	☐
☐	Fast track pass	☐
☐	Priority boarding pass	☐
☐	Online check-in reminder (add to my calendar 48 hours prior)	☐
☐	Complete check-in online / check seat allocation	☐
☐	Save boarding pass / add to calendar	☐
☐	Colour code all travel	☐
☐	Travel dates top of calendar	☐
☐	Travel docs top of cal with docs	☐
☐	Travel docs to I-Cloud drive	☐
☐	Airport transfers / contact numbers	☐
☐	Hotel check-in / check-out	☐
☐	Advise traveller when booking complete	☐

I block out the check-in time, the flight time, and the ground transfers in my exec's calendar. I complete check-in for my travellers, I download boarding passes. I then add all travel documents to the calendar in multiple places, so that my traveller can access it with ease.

The checklist I built works, and its enabled me to book with confidence, enter data into the calendar in the right order, and gives my traveller assurance, because they know I'm a professional business travel co-ordinator, and I don't miss a detail when co-ordinating their travel.

View the right hand side of the checklist. Under the subheading '**Add to Calendar**' I've created two columns, with checkboxes underneath '**flight outbound**' and '**flight inbound**'. That's because I'm adding two sets of data to the calendar. One for the outbound flight and one for the inbound. I like to tick the boxes for each flight as I go. It gives me confidence, that I've entered all the travel information to the calendar, for each flight.

ADD TO CALENDAR

Flight outbound		Flight Inbound
☐	Time zone	☐
☐	Block flight time / add flight ref no.	☐
☐	24 hour clock	☐
☐	Arrival time	☐
☐	Carrier	☐
☐	Terminal out / terminal inbound	☐

Create your own travel planning checklist. Use mine as your foundation. Build it once, use it every time your co-ordinating business travel. Missed something out? Amend it, and make sure it captures everything you need, when working on future business trips.

I should point out that I've had access to travel management companies and their online platforms for over 12 years now, but whilst they provide a corporate booking service, they only complete the basics.

A travel management company's booking agents will only follow your instructions, they won't prompt you to consider what class of travel your exec is permitted for a long-haul, or ask about their aisle or window seat preferences, or suggest you book fast track security because that airport is notorious for long queues. As an executive assistant, it's your responsibility to consider all of these components, when building a trip.

 Executive assistants provide the highest level of business travel management, and having a checklist to refer to every time, will allow you to consistently deliver meticulously planned trips.

Using the travel planning checklist example, build your own, for future trip co-ordination. Keep it to one page in length. Next time you're building a trip, print it, and fill in the blanks for: airport out, airport in, destinations and dates. Tick off each prompt, line by line, as you go. Use a brightly coloured pen, so you can see your progress at a glance.

I prefer the old fashioned method of printing it, and using a coloured pen to tick off the prompts as I go. It keeps the checklist visible on my desk, and acts as a reminder if I get distracted.

I even have different coloured plastic wallets, that I use for each trip, and I add an Avery sticky label to the front of the plastic wallet. I write the travel dates, traveller name, and destination on the label. At TP UK, I was working on an average of 6 trips at a time, and to have a checklist for each one (housed in a different coloured plastic wallet) helped me to keep organised. You can keep everything digital, but this system worked for me (and still does).

Building a travel planning checklist, may take an investment of your time, initially. However, it will save you stacks of time, whenever you're booking corporate travel, for your executive. What if you need to stop travel planning, and pick up an urgent task request? No problem! Pivot from your travel planning to your urgent task, and back again. The checklist allows you to see exactly where you've left off, and what's outstanding, for you to pick up and action. Nothing falls through the cracks.

To date, I've co-ordinated in excess of 5,000 business trips, and I use my travel checklist for every single one. It's a total lifesaver. I would be lost without it.

I have a drawer by my desk, dedicated to business travel. It houses all my coloured plastic wallets, Avery labels, and pre-printed travel planning checklists. Whenever I'm asked to co-ordinate a new trip, I go straight to that draw, pull out the materials I need, create a new wallet for the trip, and I'm ready to go.

When a trip's fully co-ordinated, and everything's in the calendar, I let the traveller know. I also tick the box at the bottom of the checklist, 'TRIP COMPLETED'. That tick is a BIG TICK. It gives me reassurance that I've covered everything possible for the trip, and that I've completed all the trip planning and all the calendar entries. No more worrying, or double checking – it's done, I can move on.

I can honestly say, that by using the travel planning checklist, I've never missed a step of trip coordination. Plus, I've never woken up in the middle of the night, worrying about a detail I might have forgotten. I put my faith into the system I've developed, my trusty travel planning checklist, and you can too.

STEP 21. Online Check-in

Completing online check-in for your exec, should definitely be on your radar. It's another pre-flight process, which occurs every time your exec flies on business, and it's something you can do on their behalf, so they don't have to. When you complete online check-in for your business traveller, they can skip the traditional check-in counter with the long snaking queue, and proceed directly to the security checkpoint (providing your exec has carry-on luggage only).

My **travel planning checklist** reminds me to complete online check-in for both flights (see snip below). I add a calendar entry to my calendar, two days in advance of the flight, to remind me to action this. I colour code the entry red, because it's critical that I complete this step for my boss.

☐   Online check-in (add reminder to my   ☐
diary 48 hours prior)

130

Completing online check-in for your business traveller, shows that you're a 'next level' EA. It prevents your exec from having to think about it, and creates a smoother transition through the airport, in a much shorter time.

 Any time saved by your executive on arrival at the airport, can be utilised more productively, such as checking emails, responding on Slack, making a call, or getting a bite to eat before they board the aircraft.

Let's look at the benefits of completing online check-in, for your executive, in more detail.

10 x Benefits of Online Check-in

1. **Efficiency:** online check-in is fast, and easy to action.

2. **Cost effective:** some airlines will charge you to check-in at the airport.

3. **Bypass the airline check-in desk:** if you've completed online check-in, and your exec only has carry-on luggage, they won't need to visit the airline desk on arrival at the airport.

4. **Minimise queue time:** there is no need for your exec to join the lengthy queue at the airline desk, they can proceed straight to the security line.

5. **Seat selection:** if you didn't complete this at the point of booking, you can complete this at check-in. Ensure your exec always gets their preferred seat on their flight. You can also check that any pre-booked seat number you requested, has been allocated correctly.

6. **Boarding pass generation:** online check-in will generate a digital boarding pass, or both passes if you're checking in the outbound and inbound flights together. These can be downloaded and saved to the calendar as attachments, and also saved to a pre-agreed shared folder

on the cloud (as back-up). Your exec can access the digital boarding passes when in transit, via their mobile phone, no need to print.

7. **Use the bag drop facility**: if your exec has luggage for the hold, they can use the bag drop facility at the airport and still skip the main airline check-in desk queue. The bag drop facility is typically a separate area near the check-in counters, and it's specifically designed for passengers who have already checked-in, and need to drop off their hold luggage.

8. **API data entry**: every airline now collects Advance Passenger Information (API) for their passengers, under strict border security control. Each airline will stipulate what they need, during online check-in. It usually includes the full passenger name, gender, date of birth, nationality, travel document type (passport), and passport details. You can upload all of this information, on behalf of your traveller, during online check-in. Have an image of your exec's passport ready, before you get to this step.

9. **Breeze through departures**: having their boarding pass ready to go, will help your exec breeze through the airport on the day they fly. It's the difference between travelling like a business travel professional, and standing in a queue full of holiday makers, that makes a big impact.

10. **VIP service**: give your exec the VIP treatment, and complete online check-in for every trip. It's an EA's task, and an unnecessary procedure for your boss to undertake themself. Make them feel like a VIP!

 Completing online check-in for your exec, means your boss arrives at the airport already checked-in to their flight. They can skip the airline check-in desk, and head straight to the security line. If your exec manages their own check-ins, encourage them to let you action this on their behalf.

When you've checked-in online, a boarding pass will be generated for the flight. This is the document that your exec needs to move through security, the departure gate, and to board the aircraft. Ensure its uploaded to the calendar for easy access.

Next time you complete this process for your boss, look at their passport expiry date. Add the expiry date to their calendar 7 months before its due to expire, and add a reminder to your calendar to renew their passport. Some countries will refuse entry if a passport is within 6 months of its expiry date.

Most airlines permit online check-in, from 24 to 48 hours before departure time, up until a few hours before departure. EasyJet is the exception to this rule, and allows online check-in from 30 days to 2 hours before the flight (thank you easyJet!). Make sure that you check-in during the permitted window, and remember, when it comes to seat selection, the earlier, the better.

3

Calendar Foundations

STEP 22. Calendar Foundations

Have you ever issued a meeting invite, on a public holiday, by accident? Or received a meeting invite, that landed on a bank holiday Monday in error? It's an easy mistake to make, but it can be avoided, by laying **calendar foundations**.

Has your boss ever asked you to reschedule a meeting, as several attendees declined the invitation, and replied with, "It's half term, I'm on leave". Oh dear. That could have been avoided. If only you'd been aware, of the half-term break, before you issued the meeting invite.

What if you forgot to add the date of the Barcelona trade show (the one your boss attends every year), to the calendar? The event is fast approaching, and you've just realised he's booked on a flight to London, that very same week! Oops. Now you've got to confess to the blunder, unpick the London flights (at a cost), and reconfigure the calendar. Laying **calendar foundations** could have prevented that situation.

Laying calendar foundations, consists of entering 3 categories of dates into the calendar. The categories are:

1. **Public Holidays** (bank /federal /national holidays)
2. **School Holidays** (not just for parents, this affects everyone)
3. **Trade Shows** (the annual conference, trade show, or expo your boss attends)

Every executive assistant needs to lay calendar foundations, to achieve calendar efficiency. Think of the calendar as a structure. It needs a strong foundation first, and then you can add your blocks of time, your recurring meetings, and your events, on top. Without a strong foundation, you're going to come unstuck.

The foundation is your building platform. It's going to support your calendar management, throughout the entire year. It's the base layer, for all the other additional layers you're going to add, for the months ahead. Get the foundations right, and you'll have a solid structure to build upon.

Laying calendar foundations early, means that your future meeting scheduling, wont clash with important events. Such as public holidays (when employees aren't working), school holidays (when the majority of colleagues take their time off), or industry events and tradeshows (which senior team members attend).

Omitting the step of laying calendar foundations, is like inviting chaos into the calendar, because you could schedule meetings across dates you should be avoiding. Plus, when the error is noticed, you'll spend time moving meetings around, to find a date that <u>does</u> work, and that means duplicating work and disrupting other calendar managers. It could all be avoided, by laying the basic foundations in the calendar.

Scenario A (a new job): You're an experienced EA, and you've just moved to a new job, with a new boss. Everything is unfamiliar to you, particularly the new calendar you've been given to manage. You don't know where to start, but the calendar seems like the most obvious place, to focus on.

Scenario B (a new year): You've been doing your current job for some time; you're well established in the role. You've got everything running smoothly, just how you like it. The end of the year is fast approaching, and you're starting to think about next year's calendar, which is pretty empty. There's a few recurring meetings visible, but not much else.

For both scenarios you'll have a **new calendar** to manage. Either because it's a new job and your taking on a new calendar, or because you're heading into a new year and it's almost a blank schedule. Both are unchartered territories, so it's vital to lay calendar foundations, in order to build the base for you to work from, effectively. Let's take a look at both scenarios in more detail:

Scenario A: You've moved jobs (perm/contractor/temp), and you've inherited an existing calendar from your predecessor, to manage. You may, or may not, have had the luxury of a handover. At first glance the calendar looks ok. Colour coding has been applied. Your exec's internal meetings include links to agendas, and actions.

The 1:1s are linking to spreadsheets with tracked actions, and the next 2 x 'Senior Leadership Team' meetings are visible. You can see an 'All Hands' approaching, and there's a client meeting next week, with a pre-meet before, and a de-brief scheduled after.

On the surface the calendar looks good. Your predecessor was good at their job (you think to yourself). But don't assume, that the calendar you've just taken over, is up to your own high standards of accuracy. Just because it's been handed over to you by another EA, doesn't mean its operationally effective, or error free.

Just think about this situation for a moment. You've been given the keys to someone else's calendar to operate. It's a bit like driving a new car, and changing from the car you're familiar with driving every day, to a different one which you don't know how to operate yet.

Think back to when you last changed your car, and the seller handed you the keys. Did you simply hop in and drive it away at full speed, without inspecting the service log, the condition of the tyres, the mileage, the history of ownership, or the oil levels? Did you place 100% trust in the previous owner, and think to yourself, "Oh it will be alright, she seemed like a really nice person!" and continue to drive it until it broke down, with smoke billowing from under the bonnet?! No, of course not, that would be illogical.

Before you drove your 'previously owned' vehicle away, you asked questions, you pressed buttons, you checked its performance, its service history, and you kicked those tyres!

You were looking for faults and defects, because you didn't want to drive it in ignorance. You didn't want to put yourself at risk of having a bad experience further down the line, and you most certainly didn't want to breakdown.

Calendar handover is exactly the same. **Don't assume the calendar's been regularly serviced, or highly maintained by your predecessor. There are basic checks to complete, before you can drive it confidently.** You need to complete due diligence, limit any potential damage, and mitigate any risks.

Laying calendar foundations, is exactly like completing the checks you'd make before driving that new car, for the very first time. Only it's the calendar structure you're checking, instead of a car. So you'll check for public holidays, school holidays, and trade shows first, to ensure the fundamental 'dates to observe' are already embedded into the schedule, before moving onto any meeting scheduling (recurring or otherwise).

attention to detail

Always ensure the calendar you're managing is roadworthy before you drive it. Just because it was managed by an EA before you, doesn't necessarily mean its fit for purpose.

Scenario B: You've had the same boss for over 1 year, it's November and you're thinking about next year's calendar. Is there much to do? Surely all the recurring meetings just do their own thing, and repeat next year. The senior leadership team meetings will be issued from above, and your executive will tell you when he's booked his vacation, or when there's a trade show he wants to attend. It will all work itself out. No need to stress over it. Life is good...

No! Don't become complacent! Calendar management is your skill, and planning for next year is what sets you apart, from your less experienced EA peers. Get ahead, and give this process the time and focus that it deserves. Moving into a New Year, without completing the basic groundwork of **laying calendar foundations**, means that you've missed the critical step of building the calendar effectively for your boss.

 Calendar foundations include the non-negotiable dates: public holidays, school holidays, industry events, and these are the dates that don't move. Respect them, or they'll be problems further down the line.

Let's work through each of the calendar foundations step by step, to ensure your calendar is roadworthy, for the year ahead. First up is public holidays. In Step 23, I'll share my tips with you, on how to automate adding public holidays to the calendar, and why you should observe international dates as well. So, buckle up, and let's get going...

STEP 23. Public Holidays

The first calendar foundations, to build into your exec's calendar, are public holidays. Also known as federal, national and bank holidays. These are **non-negotiable** annual events, and must be clearly visible in the calendar, so that you don't issue a meeting invitation on the same date, by mistake.

Imagine you're scheduling a new 'All Hands' meeting, for a couple of months' time. You've spotted a potential time and date in your bosses diary that's available, 11:00 BST on Monday 27 May. Using the shared calendars feature, you've viewed the availability of the SLT members, and the time and date is showing as free in their calendars.

You proceed and issue the 'All Hands' meeting invite from your boss's calendar, for the 27 May at 11:00 BST, which is going to all employees. You wait for the meeting acceptances to appear in your boss's inbox. But instead of seeing 'accepted' notifications, you're seeing the exact opposite. The notifications are showing as 'declined', and the comments appearing advise, "This is a Bank Holiday".

Oops. You just messed up, and issued a meeting invite to the entire company on a public holiday, and everyone's witnessed it. Oh, the shame!

But how could you have missed such an important date? The bank holiday wasn't showing in your exec's calendar! The SLT members all had 'free time' showing at the proposed time. How could this have happened? What a nightmare.

You'll have to start all over again. You'll have to reschedule the meeting to the Tuesday, if you can find a convenient slot. By moving the meeting, you're creating unnecessary email traffic for everyone in the company, and you're left with egg on your face, and that's never a good look.

Issuing a meeting invite on a public holiday is a schoolgirl error, it's a basic mistake and could have been avoided. After all, executive assistants are professional calendar managers, and lead by example.

WARNING... public / national / bank / federal holidays **are not visible** in Outlook calendars or Google calendars by default.

Yes, seriously! You have to go into the settings and import them into your calendar, to make them appear. But before you rush ahead and complete the necessary steps required, let's think about which public holidays you should import.

Where does your executive live? That's a good place to start. I'm a UK based EA, but I've previously supported execs who live in Denmark, Portugal, Austria, Germany, and the US, and all of those countries observe different public holidays to the UK. So, whilst it seems logical to import the UK holidays into the calendar, I'm actually missing the public holidays that occur in my exec's country, and those public holidays will have an impact on his availability, and his business travel. Therefore, I need to import the UK public holidays, plus the public holidays for my exec's location.

What if you're supporting an executive who is a frequent business traveller? Where do they travel to the most? Is it the US, UK, the Philippines, Ireland, Singapore or another international destination? Each of those countries observe their own public holidays. So, by adding the public holidays for those countries into the calendar, you can avoid scheduling a QBR, workshop or site visit, on a date where the 'local' employees are 'out of office', and enjoying a national holiday.

Where is your exec's line manager based? In a multinational organisation your boss's boss is likely to be based in a different country, observing a different set of public holiday dates, to your boss. Let's say your exec is based in the UK, and his or her boss is based in the US. You should add all the US holidays to the calendar (as well as the UK's) to prevent your exec contacting their boss on a federal holiday, or requesting a meeting with them on those dates.

US National Holiday Dates 2024

Date	Holiday
Monday, January 01	New Year's Day
Monday, January 15	Birthday of Martin Luther King, Jr.
Monday, February 19 *	Washington's Birthday
Monday, May 27	Memorial Day
Wednesday, June 19	Juneteenth National Independence Day
Thursday, July 04	Independence Day
Monday, September 02	Labor Day
Monday, October 14	Columbus Day
Monday, November 11	Veterans Day
Thursday, November 28	Thanksgiving Day
Wednesday, December 25	Christmas Day

The US has 11 national holidays, whilst the UK only has 8.

Where's your company's headquarters? If your company's HQ is in Paris, import France's national holidays. By doing so, you'll know when your Paris HQ is closed for business, and when your French colleagues will be 'OOO'.

Do you have colleagues and team members based internationally? Which countries are they based in? You must be aware of those public holidays too, as it helps when you're scheduling meetings with those colleagues.

No executive assistant wants to issue a meeting invite to several participants, only to receive multiple replies confirming "This is a public holiday!" Public holidays aren't visible in Outlook or Google calendars by default, you have to import them.

Use the Public Holiday Checklist below, to assess which country's dates you should import. When you know which countries you need, read on, to learn about the **'add holidays'** feature in Outlook.

Public Holiday Checklist

Which Countries do you need to import?

- ☐ Where does your exec live?
- ☐ Where's your company HQ?
- ☐ Where's your exec's line manager based?
- ☐ Where does your exec travel to frequently?
- ☐ Is your team international? Import the countries where each team member is based e.g. Singapore, Japan, Australia.
- ☐ Is your team in Europe? Whereabouts? European member states don't have the same national holidays so import each country e.g. Germany, Austria, or France.

Add Holidays with Outlook

Now that you're aware of which country's public holidays to import, **change your own calendar settings first**. Beware, you need to complete this task twice, once for your calendar, and once for your exec's calendar. If you have multiple execs, you'll need to complete this for each one.

1. Open Outlook
2. Click File > Options > Calendar
3. Under Calendar options, click 'Add Holidays'

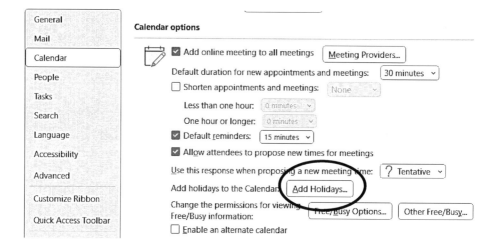

4. Check the box for each country whose holidays you want to add to your calendar, and then click OK.

Outlook will auto-populate the calendar, with the public holidays of all the locations you've selected. But, it's only going to do this for <u>your</u> calendar.

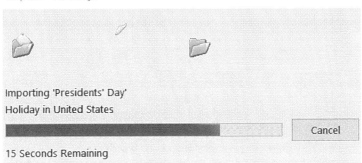

Importing 'Presidents' Day'
Holiday in United States

[Cancel]

15 Seconds Remaining

To import public holidays into **your exec's calendar**, you'll need to repeat the process directly from your exec's laptop. Unfortunately, it isn't possible to change your exec's holiday settings, from your own device. However, there is a work around. You can copy the downloaded calendar entries across from your calendar, into theirs. This is my preferred method, and I'll explain how.

Open your calendar on a 1 week view, or month view. Open your exec's calendar with the same view, so they are side by side. Drag and drop each holiday entry from your calendar, across to your exec's calendar. By doing this manually for the entire year, you'll see instantly if you have an existing meeting conflict, on the date of the public holiday you've just copied across.

Copy across all the public holidays you've imported to your calendar, over to your exec's calendar. Check for any conflicts, for all of the public holiday dates, as you drag and drop them over. Consider the impact the public holiday has on any existing meeting entries, and whether you need to reschedule any of those existing meetings.

Remember, all the public holiday dates you've added aren't always observed by your line manager. Some of them are FYI (for your information), so you won't necessarily need to clear all meeting entries from every public holiday date. For example, if you imported Australia's national holidays because you have 2 team members based in Australia, it doesn't mean that you have to clear your bosses calendar on those dates (who is based in the UK). It's just a date to be aware of (an FYI date).

However, any public holiday dates imported for the country where your executive lives and works, should definitely be blocked as 'OOO' as these are national holidays and will be observed.

For the national holidays observed by your country, change each entry in the calendar from 'free time' to 'out of office'. Double click on the entry, and use the 'Show As' button with the drop down arrow. This will prevent anyone inviting your boss to a meeting on those dates (providing they check availability first). It will also prevent you from treating the date like a standard business day, when it's a national holiday.

Add to Bible...

Update your Bible with a new section titled 'Public Holidays to Import'. List all the countries you've imported, and why, e.g. UK (my location), Ireland (Chris's team are based in Dublin), US (Group colleagues), Austria (Otto and Fritz live there) etc. Add the details to your Bible once, and refer to them next year when repeating the task.

For Google Workspace users, there isn't an option to import public holidays, but a feature does exist to allow you to **overlay** holidays onto the calendar view. I don't find this particularly helpful, because if you don't have the 'public holiday view' selected, you can't see them. My workaround to this pretty useless Google feature, is to manually add the dates.

With the public holidays imported into your calendar, and the calendars of those you support, you can move onto the next step of calendar foundations – School Holidays.

STEP 24. School Holidays

You've added all the public holidays into your calendar (and your exec's calendar), using Outlook. If you're a Google Workspace user, you've added the dates in manually. Nice job!

Public holidays are the first foundation stone of the calendar, the second is school holidays, and school holidays affect everyone. Don't skip this step if you think it's only relevant to executives who have children. The consequences of 'school holidays' are companywide, not just for parents.

School holidays affect businesses of all sizes, because substantial numbers of employees have children, and when the schools break up for holidays, parents take time off too. Either to look after their children at home, or take them on vacation.

Because school holidays are scheduled on similar dates at multiple locations, it means that high numbers of employees take their annual leave or PTO (paid time off) simultaneously. In turn, this has a big impact on business operations, meetings, and corporate events.

Does your executive have any children? If so, it's beneficial to add their school term dates to the calendar. Your exec will either want to book time off, during the school holidays, or book the dates as 'work from home'. Whatever they do, and whatever childcare arrangements they already have in place, its important the school holiday dates are visible, so you can avoid booking your exec on any international trips, during that period.

If the school holidays have already been plugged into your exec's calendar, by your predecessor, don't assume the data is accurate. Check the information yourself (kick those tyres). This is your calendar to manage, so you must start afresh, and check the accuracy of any existing details.

Spring term 2024

- Start of term: Monday 8 January, 2024

- Half term: Monday 12 February to Friday 16 February, 2024

- End of term: Thursday 28 March, 2024

- Easter holiday: Friday 29 March – Friday 12 April, 2024

Summer term 2024

- Start of term: Monday 15 April, 2024

- May day: Monday 6 May, 2024

- Half term: Monday 27 May to Friday 31 May, 2024

- End of term: Monday 29 July, 2024

England school terms for Spring/Summer 2024

School terms vary by country, so ensure you have the exact dates for your exec's children (if applicable). Ask your exec to provide you with the name of their children's school. View the school's website, and plug the school holiday details into the calendar.

I add school holidays as 'all day events', showing as free time. The entry is visible at the top of the calendar schedule, but doesn't show as busy or blocked time. If my exec decides to take the dates as leave, I then mark the date as 'OOO'.

Add to Bible…

Add your exec's children's school details to your Bible, and link the website. Schools only publish 1 years' worth of dates at a time, so you'll need to complete this exercise again next year. Add a reminder to your calendar to do just that.

Even if your exec doesn't have children, colleagues and clients will, so adding the dates of school holidays to the calendar, will be extremely useful. It will flag up when colleagues are likely to be taking their annual leave (PTO), and therefore unavailable for 1:1s, meetings, or calls.

 Create a category colour for school holidays, so that you can spot them at a glance. When you've added all school holidays for the next year into your calendar, drag and drop all of those entries across into your exec's calendar.

When you visit a school's website, you'll find they often have an 'annual school calendar' which is downloadable direct to Outlook or Google Calendars. But that's something for the 'family' calendar, and you operate the 'business' calendar (plus you'll get a load of unnecessary information downloading). You want basic school holiday dates only (the main holidays and the half terms), and that's why it's best to enter these manually.

Find a reliable website for your location's term dates. In the UK term dates are regional (England, Ireland, Scotland, Wales). Add the dates to your own calendar showing as 'All Day Event / Free', so that the date doesn't show as 'busy', then drag and drop the entries over to your exec's calendar.

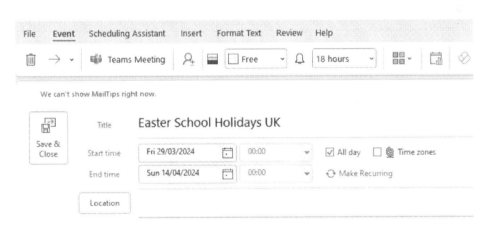

When you're completing this part of the process be vigilant. Look for any existing meetings, milestones, or company events, which may conflict with a school holiday. If you find something, you should raise the conflict with your manager, but complete the exercise for the whole year first, or you could get distracted. Better to go to your manager with a list of any conflicts, rather than raising them one by one.

 Note down any conflicts as you go, and email your exec advising that you've identified clashes with school holidays. Its fine to ask your executive for their input, because it demonstrates that you've shown 'foresight' in your calendar management. You're flagging up potential issues, long before they happen.

If your exec is based in a different country to you, or your team are international, you need to check the school vacation dates for those countries. They may correspond with the term dates for your own country, but some European member states have different school holiday 'zones', which means schools break up on different dates. The school holiday periods are staggered.

European school holiday dates can often be found on Ski websites:

Try Myskistay.com for dates with European zones

For US school holidays try Schoolholidays-usa.com

For UK school holidays try Publicholidays.co.uk/school-holidays

Adding term dates is relevant for the business, as it shows when the holiday periods fall, e.g. easter holidays, summer holidays, half terms etc. These are the periods when the vast majority of colleagues take their annual leave, to go on family holidays, or to look after their children at home.

 When scheduling companywide events such as an 'All Hands' or your 'SMKO' (Sales and Marketing Kick Off) always avoid the school holidays. This is when the majority of colleagues are going to take their PTO. You can improve attendance rates, by factoring in the school holiday break, and scheduling around it.

When the school holidays are locked into the calendar schedules, move on to the next calendar foundation – trade shows.

STEP 25. Trade Shows

Every business sector has its own annual calendar of conferences and events, which take place throughout the year. A trade show, also known as an exhibition, expo, summit, or trade fair, brings people together to showcase their products, services, and innovations. These international events provide the attendees with a face to face environment in which they can network, learn about new developments and trends, attend seminars and workshops, and meet industry leaders.

Trade shows are largescale events, lasting 1-3 days in duration, occurring once a year. You may be familiar with:

1. **Mobile World Congress** in Barcelona, Spain. This top international trade show covers robotics, telecommunications, and technology. Circa 100,000 attendees.
2. **MEDICA** in Dusseldorf, Germany. One of the largest trade shows in Europe with 120,000 visitors. Featuring pharmaceuticals, medical technology, and hospital equipment.
3. **Ambiente** in Frankfurt, Germany. Dedicated to consumer goods and retail. 100,000 attendees.
4. **Web Summit** in Lisbon, Portugal. A tech conference and trade show, previously held in Dublin, 70,000 attendees.
5. **Hannover Messe** in Hannover, Germany. 215,000 attendees coming together for manufacturing, engineering, robotics, and tech.
6. **CES (Consumer Electronics Show)** in Las Vegas. Features manufacturers, developers, technology, and new products with 150,000 attendees.

These 'business 2 business' or 'B2B' events repeat annually, and allow companies to showcase their new products and services, to existing clients and potential new clients (prospects).

Exhibiting companies (the exhibitors) enter into a contract with the show organisers, and lease a 'space' within the exhibition venue, for the duration of the trade show. Stand space varies in size, but essentially it's an empty space, which the exhibitor hires to place their trade stand (or booth) on. Exhibitors design, build, and pay for the cost of their own 'trade stand', from which they promote their goods and services to visitors.

Iron Mountain exhibition stand

Companies invest an enormous amount of time and money participating in trade shows, to showcase their latest technology and services. It takes months of planning by the marketing and events teams, to work with a designer, the head of business development, and the head of commercial, to produce a stand that's going to launch the latest innovation, and create a buzz in the marketplace.

Amongst all the various stands in the exhibition venue, there'll be dedicated conference theatres, plus smaller seminar and workshop areas. Industry experts are often asked to 'speak' at these events, and a comprehensive conference programme forms part of the trade show or exhibition's attraction to visitors.

Whatever industry you're working in, e.g. banking, finance, technology, medical, pharmaceutical, manufacturing, telecoms, or e-commerce, there'll be a prominent trade show or exhibition that's targeted to your company. Maybe it's of interest to your company as a potential exhibitor, or maybe there are several execs that wish to attend as delegates. Perhaps your boss will be approached to be a keynote speaker.

The trade shows which are key to your business executive, should definitely be added to the calendar for awareness. A good time to complete this exercise is towards the end of the current year, when the trade show dates have been published for the year ahead.

The quickest route to locating the trade shows your company already participates in, is to ask your Chief Marketing Officer (CMO), or your Head of Events, for the data. They'll know which trade shows your company exhibits at, and the ones they don't, and the ones that could be of interest to your boss.

The marketing and events professionals in your organisation, know all the trade shows in your sector, inside out. Don't waste time on completing independent research, when you can tap into expert inhouse knowledge. Reach out to your inhouse marketing and events experts, for trade show information.

A calendar of tradeshows and industry events may exist on your company intranet, SharePoint, or Google Drive. Ask a marketing and events colleague to send you a link.

When you've got the relevant trade show data, add each one into the calendar. Double click the top of the calendar schedule, and create a new event. Ensure you select 'Event / All Day / Free'. You don't want to block out your exec's time just yet, wait until their attendance is confirmed. Add a colour category to the event entry, the location, and a link to its website.

If you don't have a marketing and events team, and need to research industry trade shows and events yourself, use the helpful websites below:

www.10times.com   **www.tradefairdates.com**

www.industryevents.com   **www.eventseye.com**

Even if the executive you support doesn't attend these events in-person, you can guarantee that key people in your organisation will, along with a percentage of your existing clients. For that reason, continue to flag the trade show dates in the calendar, and you'll avoid scheduling any important internal or external events on those dates.

By flagging the dates in the calendar well in advance, your exec will know where the trade shows land in the forthcoming year, and will be able to plan their attendance ahead of time. That means you can book flights and hotel accommodation several weeks in advance, at a much better price.

Large international trade shows always push up prices of travel and accommodation significantly, so getting ahead in this respect will save your company a small fortune, and you'll get a wider range of hotel options to choose from.

Add to Bible... Create a list of trade shows, exhibitions, and conferences in your sector that your company attends every year. Add the data, together with website links, to your Bible. Name the section 'Trade Shows & Industry Events'. Use this list when you're laying your calendar foundations for the year ahead.

When you've completed this step, you've laid all 3 of the calendar foundations. Time to move on to the next section...

Midway Mastery: 10 minutes of your time

You've made it past the halfway point, of executive assistant mastery. Congratulations! You're making significant progress, and I'm thrilled to be part of your journey. Before you continue with the rest of the 43 steps, I have a few small requests:

1. **Leave a review on Amazon:** I would greatly appreciate it if you could take a moment to leave a review for my book on Amazon. Your feedback is invaluable. By sharing your thoughts, you're helping other EAs understand if this book is for them, and your comments mean the world to me.

2. **Connect with me on LinkedIn:** I publish regular posts on LinkedIn, specifically curated for EAs like you. Connecting with me will ensure that you don't miss out on the latest insights and advice. LinkedIn is where our EA community thrives, so let's stay connected and continue learning from each other.

3. **Exciting news for 2024 'online courses for busy EAs':** In 2024, I'll be launching a series of deep-dive training courses, designed for busy corporate EAs. If you're interested in knowing more about these courses, and want to be among the first to benefit from them, please reach out to me on LinkedIn.

4. **Your input matters:** I'm always eager to hear your thoughts and ideas. If you have a topic you'd like to see covered in my next book, or online course, please let me know, and together we can shape the content that truly matters to you. Email me at: mariafullermastery@gmail.com

Thank you!

Now, back to the 43 Steps…

4

Rhythm of Business

STEP 26. Rhythm of Business

Congratulations on completing the previous steps of laying calendar foundations! You've covered all the bases, and ensured that the relevant 'non-negotiable' dates are visible in the calendar, throughout the forthcoming year.

As a result, the calendars you manage are now showing public holidays, school holidays, and half terms. Plus, the trade shows and conferences your boss might attend, have been plugged in. If your company is exhibiting at a trade show or hosting a conference, those dates are marked in too for visibility.

What a sense of achievement! Laying calendar foundations, is the indisputable way of creating a solid calendar to build upon. You've put in the hard work, sourced the data, and added it to the schedule. You've demonstrated your efficiency, your pro-activeness, and your attention to detail. Fantastic!

With your calendar foundations laid correctly, you can safely move onto the next step of building an optimised and effective calendar, for your executive. To start with, its essential you understand how your company operates.

Have you ever considered in your capacity as an EA:

> ? **Why** do we do everything on a 12 month cycle?
> ? **Why** do we break things down into quarters, throughout the year?
> ? **Why** do we have 'kick off' events early in the year?
> ? **Why** are there financial reporting deadlines?
> ? **Why** is the UK financial year-end in April?

Well, it's because every business has an operating rhythm of its own, otherwise known as its **rhythm of business** or **'ROB'**. A rhythm of business refers to the regular activities and processes that a company undertakes, so it can operate effectively and achieve its goals. All companies have a set pattern of activities to keep things running smoothly, and strategic objectives to work towards. They all have a 'rhythm', which repeats throughout the year.

The **rhythm of business** includes key internal functions, such as financial reporting, SLT meetings, quarterly strategy sessions, monthly all-hands meetings, employee engagement initiatives, and other structured processes and programmes, that help a company to operate effectively. It's the 'heartbeat' of the organisation's activities.

All companies need a framework to operate effectively, whether they are at start-up phase or well established. You can't predict the future of business, but you can prepare for it. A **rhythm of business** (ROB) is a mechanism used to plan your company's key events, milestones and activities, for the forthcoming business year.

A rhythm of business keeps everything running smoothly and methodically, across all corporate functions and teams. Everyone knows when important events are happening throughout the year, when their objectives should be met, and when their performance reports must be submitted.

The company you work for, has a rhythm of business. There'll be an annual schedule of meetings, together with monthly financial reporting deadlines, to ensure that company executives are kept on track, and working towards the goals set by your organisation.

So, how does this impact the executive assistant? A company's 'ROB' depicts what happens at different times of the year, and it's down to you as the EA, to observe your company's operating rhythm and adopt it. You must ensure that the key meetings take place, at the right time of year, with the right attendees, in order to facilitate the company's goals, and to support your exec's leadership. No pressure there then!

Let's take a look at a simplified ROB:

- Senior Leadership Team meetings are held every week on Mondays
- ExCo (Executive Committee) is monthly on the last Tuesday
- Strategy Session is held quarterly, offsite
- Advisory Board is held every 6 weeks
- Product Executive Board is held every 4 weeks
- All Hands are monthly on the first Tuesday
- EMEA Board is monthly on the last Thursday

Senior level and companywide meetings don't just land in the calendar, when it's most convenient for the participants to attend. They're held at pre-determined times throughout the year, that align with the company's **rhythm of business**. The meetings are staggered at strategic points, that align with the company's financial year (also known as the fiscal year).

EAs play a crucial role in supporting their execs with the rhythm of business, by ensuring that the recurring patterns are embedded into the calendar, and are communicated to everyone involved. EAs have the responsibility of upholding the ROB, and ensuring key meetings and activities happen when they are supposed to. It's our responsibility to keep our exec on track, to ensure they're utilising the framework, and meeting the relevant deadlines.

 The rhythm of business (ROB) is also known as the governance model or operating rhythm. It's the heartbeat of your organisation, and executive assistants are pivotal to the delivery of every company's ROB, and its effectiveness.

As calendar managers, it's imperative to work in alignment with the rhythm of business for your organisation. Any meetings, company initiatives or processes that form part of your company's framework, take priority. There will be priority meetings and reporting deadlines, that should be locked into the calendar **before** you start scheduling your bosses' own meetings, (for example your bosses 1:1s and team meetings). The ROB framework comes first.

So, the ROB is going to be very impactful for you and your exec, which is why it must be adopted and respected. The next steps will equip you with how to implement your company's ROB, how to secure all the key dates and meetings, and add them to your exec's calendar. When you've completed the steps, you're exec is going to be the most organised and prepared they've ever been!

Step 27 shines a light on the term **'Fiscal Year'**. It's the fiscal year that underpins your company's rhythm of business. You'll discover the answers to the following questions:

?   What is a 'Fiscal Year'?
?   Why do I need to know about it?
?   How does it affect my executive?

Let's go...

STEP 27. The Fiscal Year

If you've completed Step 26, you're familiar with the concept of a **rhythm of business** or **'ROB'.** You understand why EAs need to support their execs, with the roll out and adoption of the **'ROB'** framework, for the year ahead.

Now it's time to locate the ROB framework for your company, and add it to the calendar. However, it's unlikely you'll find your company's rhythm of business, documented in a digital file, or excel spreadsheet. In my experience I've always had to go looking for the data, it's never been communicated to me in its entirety. But, I have the solution to this issue, and I'm going to share my methods on how to pull the key components together (the data), in order to capture the information that's relevant to your executive.

The key components of a company's rhythm of business are:

1. **Financial Reporting Deadlines**: understanding your fiscal year
2. **The Annual Meetings Schedule**: the framework of senior level meetings that repeat throughout the year
3. **Human Resource Timelines:** employee engagement initiatives, performance reviews, all driven by HR, aka the People Team

Let's begin with no.1, **the fiscal year**. Accountancy can be boring, however its critical to understand this element of basic company accounting. Please bear with me whilst I explain... it will be over soon, I promise!

Q. What is a fiscal year?

A. The fiscal year is a 12-month accounting period, that a business uses for financial and tax reporting purposes. A fiscal year, also known as a 'financial year', begins at the start of a quarter. For example, a typical **fiscal year starts** on the 1 January, or it could start on 1 April, or 1 July or 1 October.

The **fiscal year-end** date is at the end of a quarter. For instance, if your company's fiscal year begins on 1 April 2023, the fiscal year will end on 31 March 2024 (the 12 month period).

WARNING: A fiscal year can be different to a calendar year; it doesn't have to start on January 1 and end on December 31. The company you work for has chosen when their fiscal year operates, so you definitely need to understand when your company's fiscal year starts and ends.

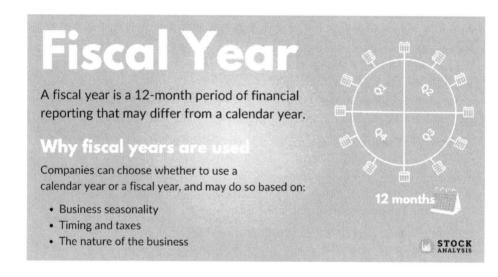

Fiscal Year

A fiscal year is a 12-month period of financial reporting that may differ from a calendar year.

Why fiscal years are used

Companies can choose whether to use a calendar year or a fiscal year, and may do so based on:

- Business seasonality
- Timing and taxes
- The nature of the business

STOCK ANALYSIS

Why is the fiscal year important in business? Why do EAs need to know about it? During the fiscal year, the finance team monitor and record all of your business' finances, including costs, profit margin and revenue. These numbers are compared with your yearly budget and goals, to determine the year's financial success.

Having a defined fiscal year or 'FY' (a fixed 12 month period), allows companies and investors, to measure performance over the year. It allows them to compare revenue and costs with previous years (year over year), and to make business decisions on investment, growth, or cutting costs.

Year over year (YOY) is a term used in accounting and financial reporting, and is used to compare a company's performance and financial data from one year to the next.

10 x Fiscal Year Responsibilities for Executive Assistants

1. **Financial Reporting:** assist in budget planning and financial reporting meeting co-ordination (month-end, year-end), and communicate any deadlines.
2. **Quarterly Reports:** support your exec by understanding what's due and when, blocking time out in their schedule to complete reports, and issuing reminders.
3. **Strategy Sessions and Workshops:** scheduling quarterly meetings, documenting agreed outcomes. Booking meeting rooms or venues, logistics.
4. **Quarterly Business Reviews (QBRs):** collaborating with your exec to prepare and schedule QBRs. Collating presentations and reports, booking a venue, logistics.
5. **Board Meetings:** scheduling the meetings, blocking calendar prep time, co-ordinating the decks, taking down actions.
6. **Performance Reviews:** co-ordinate your exec's employee performance reviews, for their team members, understanding what's required and when, communicating deadlines and actions.
7. **Expense Management:** submitting expenses on time for your exec, approving expenses, chasing team members to submit theirs. Flagging any out of policy expenses submitted, uploading matching VAT receipts.
8. **Employee Compensation:** scheduling compensation reviews, bonus sign offs, ensuring deadlines are met, collaborating with HR.
9. **Auditors and Compliance:** co-ordinating meetings, communications, and collaborating with finance on any external requirements.
10. **Kick-off Event:** support the planning and organisation of the annual kick-off event, which always lands at the beginning of the fiscal year.

The 10 points above, highlight how pivotal executive assistants are, in helping companies (and their executives) to complete essential business operations during the fiscal year, and to meet the deadlines.

Every business has its own financial deadlines to observe, within its fiscal year, and this will impact on your exec, whether they are the CEO of the company, the SVP of Business Development, or the CTO of EMEA. Understanding the fiscal year for your company, and adding in the relevant milestones to your boss's calendar, is going to help them meet their financial reporting deadlines, and to action the regular financial management tasks required of them.

 Contact your CFO or Finance Director and ask them to confirm the fiscal year period, for your organisation. Ask which financial dates (within the fiscal year) are relevant to your exec, and could they share any reporting deadlines with you. Confirm that you're keen to add all the relevant reporting deadlines into your exec's calendar, so that they don't miss anything. Add the data to your exec's calendar, with a colour category for 'finance'.

Add to Bible...

 Save the dates into your Bible. If a member of the finance team emailed them to you, just copy and paste them. Next year when you're completing the same exercise, revisit the list and ask for an updated version.

If adding financial reporting deadlines to the calendar wasn't previously on your radar, then it's something you should get into the habit of doing, as its key to your company's **rhythm of business,** and your bosses deliverables. It will also help you to prepare for the sudden flurry of financial reporting activity, at certain times of the year.

The critical thing to remember, when adding financial deadlines to the calendar, is that not all companies operate under the same fiscal year. Each individual company chooses when its fiscal year starts and ends. It's not something they have to observe, like the standard calendar year which runs from January to

December. Fiscal years are different. Whilst some businesses might choose to coordinate their fiscal year, to mirror the standard calendar year for ease of accounting, others will opt for a different set of 12 consecutive months.

This is also worth bearing in mind, when you're negotiating a new salary with a new employer. The fiscal year for a company will determine when bonus payments are made, and when annual salary reviews are completed. They don't all happen at the same time of year for every business. So, when negotiating a new job offer, you should clarify when annual performance reviews take place, because they won't necessarily be at the same time of year as your last company. Same goes for bonus payments.

Fiscal years are named using the year when the period ends. For instance, a fiscal year that runs from 1 April 2023 to 31 March 2024 is called FY24.

Collaborate with your boss on the financial reporting deadline's you've received. Ask if you should block any calendar time (before each deadline) for prep or report writing. Adding deadlines to the calendar is definitely beneficial to your boss, but blocking out time, so they can complete the work, is even more impactful.

When you know the fiscal year (start and end dates) for your company, you can figure out where the fiscal quarters fall, as they'll follow the same 12 month period. Let's look at the relevance of 'quarters' in more detail.

A company's fiscal year is broken down into **fiscal quarters** (4 x 3 month periods) and this allows for more detailed financial reporting. The fiscal quarters (simply referred to as 'quarters') will dictate when your exec should hold certain events like **quarterly business reviews** (QBRs), **quarterly strategic offsites**, and the **Kick-off event** (usually held in Q1 of the FY).

What Is a Quarter (Q1, Q2, Q3, Q4)?

A financial quarter is a 3 month period within a company's FY. It's used for financial and operational reporting and planning. Quarters help break down the financial year into manageable chunks, and provide a way to analyse the company's performance and progress, at 3 month checkpoints, throughout the year.

A quarter is one-fourth of a year, and is typically referred to as **Q1** for the first quarter, **Q2** for the second quarter, and so on. A quarter is often shown with its relevant year, e.g. Q1 2024 or Q1 24, which represents the first quarter of the FY. For example, if your company's fiscal year follows the **calendar year** of 1 Jan to 31 Dec, the quarters will look like this:

Q1: January, February, March
Q2: April, May, June
Q3: July, August, September
Q4: October, November, December

However, if your company's fiscal year follows the **UK tax year**, it will look like this:

Q1: April, May, June
Q2: July, August, September
Q3: October, November, December
Q4: January, February, March

The quarterly periods are going to determine when you hold internal events, such as your **QBR's** (quarterly business reviews) and your company **Kick-Off** (or SMKO).

Before the end of your current fiscal year, prompt your exec to start planning the QBR and the company Kick-Off for Q1. Get the dates in the calendar with the required attendees, well in advance. Other dates to add to the calendar are month-end, and year-end.

Add to Bible... Add your company's FY start and end dates, to your Bible document. Note where the quarters' fall within the year, e.g. 'Q1: April to June, Q2: July to September', and so on. Each company's FY is different, so make a note of it.

Now that your **fiscal year** is understood, you'll know when your organisation is closing its yearly financial accounts, and that means your finance team are doing a major piece of work. You can help your line manager, to help your finance team, by ensuring that all expense reports have been submitted, with corresponding receipts.

 All expense reporting needs to be closed at year-end. Help your exec to achieve this, by prompting your team to submit their expenses and receipts on time, every month. Set yourself calendar reminders to action this, and block time to complete your own expenses, and your executives, on a monthly basis.

STEP 28. Annual Meetings Schedule

An **annual meetings schedule** is a framework of senior level meetings, that repeat throughout the fiscal year. It's a structured plan, outlining all of the top tier meetings within an organisation for the next 12 months. The framework of meetings forms the company's operating rhythm, or rhythm of business. The document acts as a key reference point for executive assistants, senior level executives, and anyone who is submitting reports to the meeting co-ordinator. The annual meeting schedule, which is either a Word or Excel file, will include the following:

- Meeting name
- Date
- Location (onsite or online details)
- Start time
- Duration
- Time zone
- Attendees

The details are in summary form only, and won't necessarily list all of the attendees by name. For instance, an annual meeting schedule for a large multinational will show the attendees by group e.g. 'UK Board Members', 'EMEA Sales and Marketing VPs', 'ExCo', 'Country Heads' or whatever abbreviations your company is using.

An **annual meetings schedule** is an essential mechanism for ensuring that a company's senior level meetings are planned, organized, and communicated effectively. It gives an overview of which c-level meetings are happening throughout the year, who's required to attend, and when.

It also acts as a calendar manager's point of reference, because you know which key dates are already committed to high level meetings, and subsequently you know which dates to avoid, when scheduling your own meetings and events.

At the very top of a global organisation sits a global CEO, and the CEO's office will issue an **annual meetings schedule,** towards the end of the calendar year (for the forthcoming year). The master document will detail all the executive meetings at the very highest level in the organisation, for the next 12 months. The completed schedule will be distributed to the meeting attendees, and their EAs only.

Sometimes the CEO's office will issue the corresponding meeting invites direct from Outlook, but they might not. It really depends on the size of your organisation, and the number of attendees involved. If the scheduling involves vast numbers of attendees across multiple countries or regions, the likelihood is that only the master document will be circulated at the end of the year, and it's down to individuals (or their EAs) to block the relevant meeting dates in their own calendars

Actual meeting invitations with joining instructions will likely follow on separately, at a later date, when the meeting co-ordinator has had more time to work through all the details. Take a look at the annual meetings schedule on the following pages. It was previously issued from the CEO's office, of a global organisation with over 400,000 employees.

Annual Meetings Schedule

Location	Date	Meeting Name	Start time/zone
		January	
Online	Friday, January 11th	Executive Overview Call (EOC)	09:00 EST
Miami	Friday, January 25th	EOC	09:00 EST
February			
Online	Friday, February 8th	TPDS + TLS + GN	11:00 EST
Online	Monday, February 11th	Iberico – LatAm Board Meetings	13:00 EST
Paris	Wednesday, February 13th	EMEA Board Meetings	14:00 CET
Online	Friday, February 15th	UK Strategic Meeting	10:00 GMT
Paris	Wednesday, February 27th	Group Board Meeting	14:00 CET
Paris	Thursday, February 28th	Investor Conference	10:00 CET
March			
Miami	Friday, March 15th	EOC	09:00 EST
April			
Miami	Friday, April 26th	EOC	10:00 EDT
May			
Online	Friday, May 10th	TPDS + TLS + GN	11:00 EDT
Miami	Monday, May 13th	Iberico – LatAm Board Meetings	13:00 EDT
Miami	May 16th	EMEA Board Meetings	10:00 EDT
Paris	May 29th	Group Board Meeting	13:00 CEST
Paris	Friday, May 31st	AGM	10:00 CEST
June			
Online	Friday, June 7th	EOC	09:00 EDT
July			
Miami	Thursday, July 11th	EOC	10:00 EDT
Paris	Tuesday, July 30th	Group Board Meeting	11:00 CEST

August			
Online	August 24th	EOC	14:00 BST
September			
Online	September 12th	TPDS + TLS + GN	15:00 BST
Miami	Monday, September 16th	Iberico – LatAm Board Meetings	09:00 EDT
Miami	Wednesday, September 18th	EMEA Board Meetings	09:00 EDT
TBC	Friday, September 20th	UK Strategic Meeting	12:00 BST
October			
London	Thursday, October 10th	Benchmark and Budget Delivery	09:00 BST
November			
Online	Friday, November 8th	TPRS + TVS + GM	14:00 GMT
Miami	Monday, November 11th	Iberico – LatAm Board Meetings	09:00 EST
Miami	Wednesday, November 13th	EMEA Board Meetings	10:00 EST
Paris	Thursday, November 28th	Group Board Meeting	11:00 CEST
December			
Online	Friday, December 13th	EOC	09:00 EST

 The **annual meetings schedule** ('**AMS**') is issued by the CEO's office. It communicates the dates of the executive level meetings, for the next 12 months, to key people within the organisation. The company's EAs are responsible for blocking time in their execs calendar, until the meeting invites are received.

The **annual meetings schedule** document and its content will act as the backbone, for all senior leadership activity. The schedule is to be treated with respect, as it no doubt took great pains for the CEO's EA to produce. Due to the importance of the meetings, and the seniority of the attendees involved, the meeting dates seldom move after they've been communicated. **The dates are set in stone.**

By keeping the dates in a fixed position, it allows attendees to pre-plan and book any travel or accommodation, well in advance. Thereby obtaining the better rates and reducing their travel costs.

 Collaborate with your EA peers, to learn who issues the annual meetings schedule, in your organisation. When do they issue it, and how? Is it shared via email or is it published via SharePoint. Is there a distribution list, are you on that list?

If the annual meetings schedule document hasn't been forthcoming, approach the Chairman's or CEO's office and request it. It's very important that you obtain this, as this builds the structure for your exec's calendar, and is integral to your company's rhythm of business.

When you have access to your company's meeting schedule, view the file and highlight all the meetings your exec is required to attend. If it isn't obvious from the document itself, make time to go through this with your boss. Next, manually enter corresponding time blocks into your executive's calendar, to hold the time, until the meeting invites have been issued from the meeting co-ordinator.

Add to Bible... Add the high level meetings your boss attends in your Bible,
 together with a note confirming you've blocked the time, but are awaiting the invites. Include who issued the annual meetings schedule, and how. This will act as an aide memoire for next year.

If any key information is missing (an online meeting link, or an onsite meeting location) enter a reminder into your calendar, to chase that information down.

The annual meetings schedule will also list regional or group board dates, which your exec perhaps doesn't attend, but does submit a report for. You should add those dates into the calendar as well, as a reminder for you and your boss.

Your exec's priority meetings are now confirmed, and in the calendar. Block out any meeting prep time for your boss, and any deadlines for report submissions to the calendar.

When you've accessed your company's AMS, and blocked all the relevant dates and times out in your exec's calendar, your one step closer to embedding the rhythm of business framework firmly into your exec's schedule. The entries you've inserted into the calendar are going to keep your exec informed, organised, and prepared. You're making excellent progress!

WARNING: do not start scheduling your exec's own framework of meetings (their 1:1s and team meetings) until you've got the AMS locked into the calendar. Let's look at the reasons why, in Step 29.

STEP 29. Hierarchy of Annual Scheduling

The annual meeting schedule (or AMS) is a method used by companies, to communicate their framework of senior level meetings, for the next 12 months. It forms part of the company's rhythm of business. EAs play an important part in the rollout and adoption of this initiative, as explained in Step 28. The AMS is crafted by the CEO's EA, in collaboration with senior level stakeholders (the SLT and their EAs, Chief of Staff). When the document has been approved, it's shared via email, and published via SharePoint or Google Drive.

When received by EAs, its implemented from the top of the business down, and it creates a cascade effect. All the executive assistants view the annual meeting schedule, and block out the meetings relevant to his or her boss. The meeting co-ordinator will follow up with calendar invites. The key thing is to hold the time, as soon as the dates have been communicated.

When the CEO's office publishes the details of the top tier meetings, it gives other EAs in the business the 'green light' to commence their own annual scheduling. A scheduling **'hierarchy'** is observed. You can consider this to be EA etiquette or protocol, but the process mirrors the organisational hierarchy. Instructions are communicated from the highest level, and they are adopted and implemented by those lower down. A structure is formed.

As soon as the executive level meetings are confirmed (by the CEO's EA) the EAs below can commence working on their bosses scheduling, the team meetings, the 1:1s, the weekly catch-ups and so on. This is how senior level meetings are scheduled in a large organisation, from the top level down, in a hierarchical structure.

So how does this affect you, and your boss? Well, the **scheduling hierarchy** is to be respected, and you shouldn't issue your bosses recurring meetings, until you've got the executive level meetings locked into your boss's calendar.

Meetings issued from the top level of a business usually take priority, and if your exec is invited you accept the invites.

As a rule, executive level meeting dates don't move. When you've got those dates locked in, you can start working on the recurring meetings your exec wants with their team (their direct reports). And when those meetings are locked in, those individuals (the direct reports) can start working on the meeting framework they want to put into place, with their own teams. And so the annual meeting scheduling cascades down the tiers of the business, driven by the organisational hierarchy.

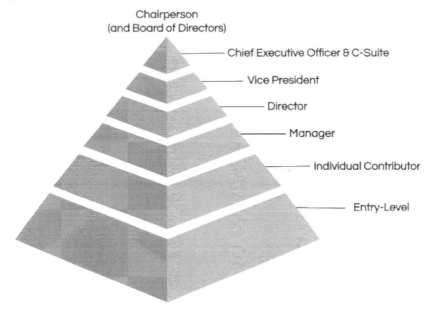

View the pyramid above. This is a great example of the hierarchy operating within an organisation. If your exec is the COO, and reports into the CEO of the company, your exec is operating at C-Suite within the business. He or she will be required to attend the top tier meetings within the company, that are relevant to their role, e.g. the Board Meetings, SLTs, QBRs, and strategy workshops etc.

Every one of those top tier meetings will have its own cadence, and will likely occur monthly for 3-4 hours duration at a time. Because of the importance of those meetings, and because they are a priority for your boss, you ensure they are locked into the calendar BEFORE you start co-ordinating and issuing any recurring meeting invites, from your boss's calendar.

If your exec is a VP (the level below C-Suite), the hierarchy still applies. VPs report into C-Suite, so you need the meeting dates your VP is required to attend, which are issued by the level above. Lock in those dates BEFORE you commence your own annual scheduling of recurring meetings, for your boss and their team.

 If you're employed by a large corporate, or a multinational organisation, your exec's calendar will be driven from the top down (like the pyramid). It will need to be structured around any senior level meetings issued from the tier above. By observing the hierarchy of annual scheduling, you'll get the senior level meetings locked into place **before** you start working on any recurring meetings for your boss, therefore avoiding any conflicts.

WARNING: always observe the hierarchy of annual meeting scheduling. This is standard EA protocol, ignore this at your peril. If you choose **not** to observe the hierarchy, and issue your exec's meetings without waiting, you'll have problems and likely end up with multiple meetings that conflict. Save yourself the bother and wait.

 The CEO's EA will communicate the annual meeting schedule. Wait for it to be issued, before you start working on recurring meetings for your boss. It's important that EAs collaborate on implementing the AMS and observe the hierarchy, otherwise it creates headaches all around.

The final component of your company's rhythm of business, is locating and embedding human resource timelines, into your exec's calendar. This involves working with a different corporate function, your HR Team (or People Team). Step 30 takes a closer look.

STEP 30. Human Resource Timelines

The Human Resources department (or People Team) are responsible for a number of critical business functions in your organisation:

- ✓ Recruiting, hiring, and retaining talent
- ✓ Onboarding and Offboarding
- ✓ Employee engagement
- ✓ Performance management
- ✓ Compensation and benefits
- ✓ Training and development
- ✓ Workplace safety, compliance, and legal issues
- ✓ Diversity and inclusion
- ✓ HR analytics and reporting
- ✓ Policies and administration

Your HR team will have an operating rhythm or **rhythm of business** of their own, to ensure that key objectives such as employee engagement activities, and employee performance reviews, happen at the right time of year, and some of those objectives will be relevant to your executive.

Your executive (in their capacity as line manager) will be required to complete regular performance management reviews with their team, and it's the timelines for those reviews that need adding to your exec's calendar. There will be mid-year reviews, end-of-year performance reviews, and setting objectives, for each of their direct reports.

Every one of these HR initiatives requires meeting scheduling, preparation time blocking out, and time for your exec to complete and upload their performance updates onto the HR platform. Understanding the timelines for these tasks, and when they should be completed throughout the year, is essential.   It's imperative not to underestimate the amount of time needed by your exec, to complete everything that's required of them by HR. Which is why you need to give special attention to this process and the timelines imposed.

A **timeline** is a period of time assigned to complete a specific task, from start to finish. Performance management timelines are issued by HR, and will need to be observed by your line manager. For mid-year and end-of-year reviews there may be a 2 week timeline, with a start date and an end date. Your exec will need to complete all activity required by HR, within that 2 week time frame.

We add the timelines for these companywide initiatives to the calendar for visibility, and to flag the window when employee evaluations and reviews should start and finish. It helps us to avoid scheduling conflicts, and it ensures it's on our boss's radar, long before the reviews are actually due. No executive wants to be the person that's being chased by an HR representative, to complete a series of performance reviews that's long overdue!

Remember, your exec is not only a senior level executive, they're also a line manager of several people. If, like me, your supporting the CEO of your company, your exec could have anything from 4 to 10 direct reports. Let's say your exec has a total number of 8 direct reports, which is about average. That could be the CFO, COO, Head of People, EVP Business Development, EVP Client Services, CTO, Head of Security & Compliance, and the CPO. That's 8 senior level executives that report directly into your line manager, plus you. So that's a total of 9 employees, your executive has line management responsibility for.

Over the next 12 months, each of those employees will need a mid-year performance review, an end-of-year performance review, an annual salary review, and a bonus review. And if their new to the business, a probationary period review, after 3 or 6 months. As a group, they may require a quarterly manager's workshop, that's driven by the requirements of HR. This is in addition to the regular recurring meetings you schedule for your boss, such as the 1:1s, weekly team meetings and regular catchups, which we'll focus on later.

Multiply all of the above performance meetings by 9 (or the number of your executive's direct reports) and that's a lot of meeting time required to complete HR procedures, on top of an already busy schedule.   All of the performance reviews, whether they're mid-year or end-of-year, will have a designated timeline for completion, which must be met by your exec. This is to ensure that everyone's reviews happen at the same time across the company, and they don't slip into the next quarter.

HR has an annual programme of performance management activities. They have their own deadlines to meet, and cut off points for line managers. Telling an HR colleague that your boss can't complete the next round of performance reviews on time, because they're hosting a client event across those dates, or travelling on business, just won't cut it.

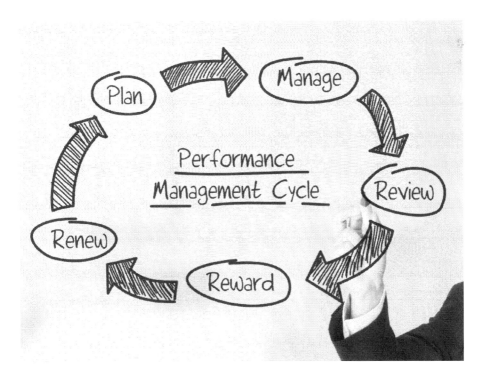

The key is to be proactive, and seek out the timelines from the HR team, well in advance. They know where the mid-year reviews will land in the fiscal year, and they know when the end-of-year reviews should take place. The deadlines are definitely on their radar, so they should be on yours too. **Don't wait for these dates to be communicated out by HR, go and find them.**

Imagine you don't know when the mid-year reviews are supposed to take place. Suddenly you get a 'Slack' message from your boss, saying the deadline to complete all mid-year reviews is 10 days away, and could you please schedule 30 minute meetings on this topic, with each of their direct reports. That's 4½ hours' worth of meetings to schedule at short notice, and before the deadline date.

Prior to those meetings, your exec needs time to complete written reviews for each direct report, and they need to be uploaded onto the HR platform. Your boss has asked you to block out 30 mins of time, per person, to complete this task. So that's an additional 30 mins of time required to write the reviews for each individual, prior to the review meetings. That's another 4½ hours of time to find, when the calendar is already full. It's going to take some calendar mastery to shuffle your exec's existing commitments around, to get 9 hours' worth of meetings, and task time, into the calendar before the HR deadline.

What if your exec is scheduled to travel to the US for a 4 day business trip, during the next 10 days? It makes it extremely difficult to fit in the mid-year review meetings, plus the written review time, and meeting the HR deadline is suddenly looking impossible. What a catastrophe! This nightmare scenario could have been avoided by pre-planning, seeking out the information in advance, and adding relevant HR timelines into the calendar.

HR, or the People Team, drive the annual schedule for line manager's deliverables, and will know exactly what your boss needs to do and when. They'll communicate what's required of your manager, directly to your manager. However, you'll probably be omitted from that conversation, so to help your manager to manage his or her team, be proactive and request the HR timelines relevant to your exec.

Every company operates slightly differently, and also uses different terminology for their in-house HR processes. But the objectives and framework, set by the People Team for their line managers, are mostly the same. The timelines will also be following your fiscal year, in terms of where the reviews land in the calendar.

 Collaborate with your HR team, and explain that you're the calendar manager for your executive. Ask them for any HR timelines that your line manager should be aware of, e.g. mid-year reviews, end of year reviews, etc. Explain that you'd like to get these dates into the calendar for visibility, well in advance, to avoid any scheduling conflicts or last minute panics.

By reaching out and requesting this information, your also strengthening your network with your HR colleagues, and cross functional relationships are hugely beneficial. Your HR team will work with you, on what's relevant for your executive, and will be pleased that you've taken the initiative to plan well in advance. Make sure you ask a senior level HR team member for the information. Go to the very top. All annual dates are agreed and communicated by the most senior person in that business area, so go direct to that HR person (or their EA) to ensure you get the most accurate and relevant data.

Additionally, you may unearth something you hadn't anticipated which you could support with, such as an employee engagement event, or an offsite event for the team. Being pro-active in this respect, also ensures that your line manager will set an example to their team. By completing employee reviews on time, and with plenty of notice.

When I supported Alistair (the CEO of Teleperformance UK), he led a series of employee engagement events, at 10 different operational sites, across the UK and Ireland. The timeline to complete those companywide initiatives was 2 weeks from start to finish, and that took some expert logistics planning!

Thankfully, I had an excellent channel of communication with Laura (the HR Director), and I was informed of the initiative well in advance. I added the timelines to the calendar, which meant I had clear visibility of what my CEO was required to action and when. I planned the logistics well in advance, and also factored in several client facing meetings at the locations he was travelling to, to maximise his time on the trip.

By **pairing** the employee engagement trip with client meetings, on the same dates and at the same locations, I'd avoided the need for a second trip by the CEO at a later date. Therefore saving the company additional travel costs, and saving my CEO time.

By adding HR timelines to the calendar well in advance, I'd not only scheduled the employee engagement events, within the timeframe and with plenty of notice, but I'd also **paired the trip** with client meetings at each location, which maximised the CEO's time.

Add to Bible...

Enter the HR activities your exec is required to complete, into your Bible. Note each process required, the time of year, the timeline set by HR, and the prep time you blocked out in the calendar for your exec. Add the contact details of the HR team member, who communicated the deadlines.

Adding HR timelines to the calendar completes the **rhythm of business** section! If you've completed all the steps in this section, your exec's calendar will contain all financial reporting deadlines, all priority meetings from the annual meeting schedule, and all HR timelines for performance management initiatives. With this content locked into the calendar, you've created a rock solid foundation from which to build upon. Fantastic!

Your exec will never miss a reporting deadline or experience a calendar conflict with a priority meeting again, **thanks to you**, and your exemplary executive assistant skills!

So, take a breather and reflect on all the positive changes you've brought about. Treat yourself to that piece of lemon drizzle cake you've had your eye on from your local café, or enjoy your favourite smoothie with a shot of golden syrup. You've earnt it!

5

Meeting Cadence

STEP 31. What is Meeting Cadence?

Meeting cadence refers to a consistent pattern of recurring meetings, that occur regularly in your organisation. To put it simply, **meeting cadence is the 'Who, What, Where, When and Why' of meeting scheduling, for recurring meetings.** It's the term used to describe a pattern or rhythm of meetings within your business, and how they land in the calendar.

When you establish a new meeting cadence with your exec, you'll agree:

- ✓ who the participants are
- ✓ the location (online or in-person)
- ✓ the duration (30 mins, 1 hour)
- ✓ the meeting purpose
- ✓ the frequency (bi-weekly, weekly, fortnightly, monthly, quarterly)
- ✓ the subject name to be used in the calendar invite

When a meeting cadence is agreed, the recurring meeting invites can be issued. This lets everyone know when the meetings are happening, and the time is secured in everyone's calendars.   If a meeting room is required, you can book one on your internal system, for the entire meeting series.

Establishing meeting cadence is efficient, because attendees are forewarned of the meeting dates (for the remainder of the year), and understand when their input is required, well in advance.

Meeting Cadence versus Rhythm of Business

Meeting cadence is similar to the rhythm of business (which sets out a framework for all the exec level meetings and events in your company, for the year ahead). A rhythm of business refers to your company's operating rhythms over a 12 month period, whereas meeting cadence refers to the frequency and format of a specific meeting series.

What is Meeting Cadence?

Implementing meeting cadence, establishes a consistent rhythm in your exec's calendar, for all the different meeting topics. It communicates expectations of the attendees, and it facilitates regular meetings for the people involved.

 A rhythm of business focuses on your company's operational framework including multiple meetings, deadlines, and activities for the year ahead. Whereas meeting cadence refers to a particular meeting series, and how its structured.

Any meeting can have a cadence. For instance, your boss could attend:

- **Company Board Meetings:** monthly, in-person, in the London office, on the last Thursday of the month, for 3 hours duration, includes all UK board members. That's a meeting cadence.
- **1:1s with their Team Members:** weekly, for 30 mins, individually, online using Zoom. That's a meeting cadence.
- **Weekly Team Meetings:** on Mondays at 10:00, using Zoom, for 1 hour, hosted by your exec with all of their direct reports, including you. That's another meeting cadence.

There are many more examples I could use, but all of the above are examples of established meeting cadences, already operating within a business.

Establishing meeting cadence, and issuing a meeting series for the year ahead, should be the default of the calendar manager (i.e. you). There are many benefits for everyone involved, in scheduling a series of meetings for the next 12 months, versus scheduling them one by one or 'whenever you need them'. Step 32, deep dives into the many benefits of setting up meeting cadence.

Time management is the obvious benefit for the meeting scheduler (the EA), when a meeting cadence is established. Afterall, why would you spend time co-ordinating and scheduling the same meeting, on a month by month, or week by week basis. When instead you could agree the meeting cadence with your exec, and schedule the entire series for the rest of the year? It's a no brainer.

To establish a new meeting cadence, for your executive, use the **5 x W's Rule**, and ask them to confirm the following:

Who?   The names of the meeting participants

What?   The subject name of the meeting series

Where?   Is the meeting location online or in-person

When?   Frequency, and when in the week/month it should land

Why?   Type of meeting and purpose e.g. team meeting, client review, 1:1, specific project etc

Recurring meetings usually fall into types or categories, and each type operates with a similar frequency. Take a look at the table on the next page. View the **Meeting Type** column on the left, it shows similar types of meetings together. On the right **Meeting Frequency** shows how often those types of meetings take place. For example, stand-ups, check-ins, and huddles, often happen **daily** in organisations. Whereas board meetings, advisory boards and offsites are often

What is Meeting Cadence?

held **quarterly**. Familiarise yourself with the types of meetings, and the frequency for each one. Does this look familiar to your exec's calendar?

Meeting Type	Meeting Frequency
Stand-ups , Team Check-ins, Agile Meetings, Water coolers, Huddles.	**Daily** Often used by start-ups, product development teams, remote teams.
Executive Meetings, Leadership Teams, Product Development, Project Status, Team Meetings, 1:1s, Catch-ups, Team Syncs.	**Weekly** Commonly used for progress, teams syncs, and forecast meetings.
All Hands, Senior Leadership Team, Board Meetings, Management Teams, Department Syncs, Project Meetings.	**Monthly** Management level check-ins and reviews. Companywide communications and updates.
Committee Meetings, Advisory Boards, Quarterly Business Reviews, Management Team Offsites, Business Development Workshop, Strategy Meetings, Strategic Planning, Customer Success.	**Quarterly** High level overview of business operations, client services reviews for the past 3 months. Regular 3 month planning, quarterly checkpoints.

A meeting's **frequency** will often be dictated by its **type**, and its purpose.

 Meeting cadence is the 'Who, What, Where, When and Why' of meeting scheduling, for recurring meetings. It's the term used to describe a pattern or rhythm of meetings within your business, and how they land in the calendar..

View the image on the next page. See how the team's recurring meetings flow throughout the week.

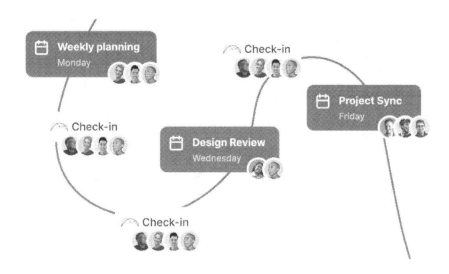

Recurring Meetings: view the terms below to describe how often meetings are held.

Daily	Everyday
Bi-weekly	Twice a week (and confusingly also means every 2 weeks) always ask your boss for clarity when scheduling
Weekly	Once a week
Fortnightly	Every 2 weeks
Bi-Monthly	Twice a month (and also confusingly every two months)
Monthly	Once a month
Quarterly	In business a quarter is a 3 month period, so quarterly is once every 3 months
Annually	Once a year

STEP 32. Benefits of Meeting Cadence

Meeting cadence is critical for running successful meetings throughout the year, as its sets expectations for the people involved. The right meeting cadence can increase productivity, and team effectiveness. However, the wrong meeting cadence can have a detrimental effect to the business, and hinder the delivery of company objectives.

Imagine your collaborating with your exec, on hosting a product demonstration followed by a dinner, to a group of external EMEA CTOs. There's a lot to organise, and you've got the support of the marketing and events team. But there isn't a weekly meeting in the calendar on this topic, and your exec hasn't asked for one.

Currently the different teams involved are emailing you with their event updates, and in turn your updating your boss on progress during your weekly 1:1. Initially this was ok, but you've just realised that the event deadline is looming, the invitations still haven't been signed off, and the guest list hasn't been approved. It's all taking far too long.

Because you don't have a regular meeting cadence in place, its having a negative effect on the event preparation. Email updates are going round and round amongst all the different event stakeholders, and you're getting caught in the middle of it all.

The solution is to be proactive, and explain to your boss that you're going to issue a 'CTO Event Planning' meeting invite, to the event stakeholders. To take place bi-weekly (2x a week) for 30 mins, in the run up to the event. By communicating a meeting cadence to the stakeholders, they'll know when the group connects, and when they'll get your boss's focus and input. Emails on this topic will reduce, because the group will wait for the meeting, to share their updates and to ask questions. Setting a meeting cadence will be more efficient, everyone will be more productive, with faster results.

Establishing a meeting cadence (for any meeting topic) sets out a meeting rhythm for your exec and their team. They'll know when certain meetings are taking place throughout the year, and on which date. They'll know the duration of that meeting, and how often it repeats. A meeting cadence also gives attendees visibility of where a certain meeting lands in the week, and allows them to plan their own meetings around it.

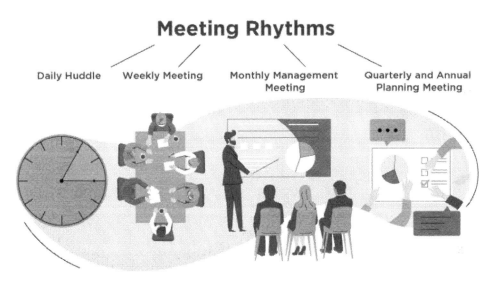

Meeting Rhythms

Daily Huddle   Weekly Meeting   Monthly Management Meeting   Quarterly and Annual Planning Meeting

A calendar that lacks meeting cadence is disorganised. Meetings will only 'happen' when a topic becomes a priority, and too many meetings at short notice can cause stress.

On the flipside, a well-managed calendar has a framework. It's been pre-planned and structured with recurring meetings, that helps your exec to meet their objectives, manage their team, and give their input to ongoing projects on a regular basis.

Let's take a look at the impact of a calendar **without cadence,** versus one **with cadence**, in more detail.

Your Executive's Calendar

Without Cadence	versus	With Cadence
Chaos!	Vs.	Order
Existing meetings move around to accommodate new requests	Vs.	Organised structured framework for pre-arranged meetings
Direct reports keep asking for catch-ups, as regular 1:1s aren't scheduled	Vs.	Direct reports know when their 1:1 meetings are, and can prepare in advance
Direct reports who request 1:1 time, get calendar time with their exec	Vs.	Equal 1:1 time given to **all** direct reports
Direct reports who don't ask for 1:1 time, don't get calendar time with their exec	Vs.	Regular check-ins scheduled with all team members means good communications
Constant juggling to meet meeting demands as they arise	Vs.	Time is scheduled for priority meetings in advance
Out of control	Vs.	Pre-planned
Time consuming for the calendar manager to react to constant meeting move requests	Vs.	With cadence established, meetings don't move around as much, which means less calendar management for the EA
A reactive calendar where the content owns the manager, and the manager doesn't own the content	Vs.	A strategically planned calendar containing the priority meetings for your executive, at the right frequency duration, and with the correct attendees

Tracking Meeting Actions

Meeting cadence is an effective tool for all managers. Its good time management, plus **the meeting rhythm can be used as a mechanism for tracking any actions agreed**. For instance, your line manager holds a weekly team meeting, you join the meeting as part of the team, plus you've been tasked to record the actions. You use a pre-prepared Excel spreadsheet to record the actions, during the team meeting. You update the 'actions' column with any agreed actions, and the name of the person who got the action. You've also added a column for 'action status'. This has a drop down box with 2 options named 'open' or 'closed'.

Immediately after the meeting, you save the spreadsheet on the company Drive or SharePoint, and you email a link to it, to all of the meeting attendees. Your team members have edit rights to the file, and they can change the action status to 'open' or 'closed'. They've already been encouraged to update their own action status, before the next team meeting.

One week later and the team meeting takes place again. The first point on the meeting team Agenda is to 'Review previous Actions'. Your exec shares his or her screen during the call, and opens the Excel spreadsheet. Immediately everyone is looking at the 'Action Status' column of the spreadsheet. Who has completed their actions, and who hasn't?

Your exec runs through last week's actions quickly, line by line, calling out the status of each one. Any 'closed' actions are acknowledged with a thank you. For any actions showing as 'open' there's a pause. Your exec calls out the person's name next to it, for an explanation. That individual suddenly has the spotlight on them, and they have to explain why they haven't completed it, in front of everyone else on that call.

You might think this practise is a bit harsh, but it's an effective management technique, to ensure that everyone completes their actions on time. Everybody had sight of the action tracking spreadsheet, immediately after the last call, and they all knew the next meeting was in 1 weeks' time. There's no room for excuses.

The key takeaway is that you don't have to chase people, to complete their actions prior to regular calls, because meeting cadence combined with an action tracking spreadsheet will do the job for you.

Chasing agreed 'actions' can be a thing of the past for EAs, when meeting cadence and an action tracking spreadsheet are combined. Attendees know the date of the next meeting, and they know which actions they were assigned. They know that the next meeting will begin by your exec reviewing the previous actions. This means you don't have to chase people up to complete their actions, because meeting cadence has already done this for you.

Attendees know they have until the next meeting to complete their actions. There are no justifiable excuses to have missed the deadline, or to join the call unprepared. They know the cadence.

EAs should establish the correct meeting cadence, for all of their exec's repeat meetings. This will improve productivity and effectiveness. We'll cover how to do that in Step 35.

Before we get into the practical element of establishing meeting cadence, let's take this opportunity to explore the acronyms and terms used, when issuing meetings. Afterall, if you're going to optimise the calendar, you need to understand the terminology first. In Step 33 you're going to demystify the acronyms, and master the unique language of meetings.

STEP 33. Meeting Terminology and Acronyms

Do you know your 1:1s from your skip levels? Your mop-ups from your huddles? And your seminars from your summits? Welcome to the wonderful world of meeting terminology and acronyms!

Business meetings have their own unique identifiers. Some are self-explanatory, and others really do need explaining. Use the glossary below to learn the definitions. Impress your boss with your expert meeting vocabulary.

Term / Acronym	Definition
1:1	1:1s are a weekly or fortnightly meeting that an employee has with their line manager. It's dedicated time for the employee to talk through their work issues, progress, challenges, and seek guidance from their boss. Also referred to as 1:1s, 1-1's, 121s, one-on-ones, and one-to-one meetings. The duration is usually 30-60 minutes. For new reports the duration is often 1 hour, then reduces to 30 mins when the new employee is established.
Action Item	An action item is a task, that's assigned to one or more meeting participant.
Agenda	A list of items, that will be covered during a meeting. Items are set out numerically in the order in which they'll be covered. The purpose of an agenda is to provide structure to the meeting, an outline of what will be discussed, and initials will indicate who will lead each numbered point.
All-Hands Meeting	An all-hands meeting includes everyone in the company, from C-level to interns, and those in between. The purpose is to provide company updates, and allow attendees to ask presenters questions. They often happen on a monthly basis, and are presented by senior level execs within the business.
Annual General	An annual general meeting (AGM) is a yearly gathering of a company's shareholders. At an AGM, the directors of the company present an annual report, containing information

Meeting (AGM)	for shareholders, about the company's performance and strategy.
Any Other Business (AOB)	An item on the agenda (usually the last) that provides an opportunity for those present, to suggest additional matters for discussion.
APAC	APAC (Asia and the Pacific) is an acronym used by global companies to describe a specific geographical area. APAC includes Australia, China, India, Japan, Malaysia, New Zealand, Russia, Singapore, and Turkey, amongst others. You may see this referred to, in regional updates and board meetings, by large multinationals.
Apologies	Giving formal notification of someone's inability to attend a meeting.
Attendance	Being present at the meeting. Attendance is often recorded in minutes or actions.
Attendees	Individuals who are invited to participate in the meeting.
Availability	Establishing who is available (and when) for a meeting, before you schedule it.
Board Meeting	A formal meeting of the board of directors, of a company or organization. The purpose is to review company performance, discuss issues, address major problems, and perform the legal business of the board.
Board Portal	A secure software application or platform, designed explicitly for facilitating communication and sharing confidential documents, between directors and senior level stakeholders. Board meeting documents are uploaded onto the portal, for secure access and collaboration.
Breakout Groups	During a large meeting or workshop, the facilitator may assign the group to work in smaller teams to answer a question, or tackle a specific challenge.
Briefing	A meeting prior to a client or supplier meeting, where instruction is given to internal attendees, and strategy is agreed.
Cadence	Meeting cadence is a consistent pattern (or rhythm) of meetings, that are pre-scheduled over a set period of time
Catch-Up	The catch-up meeting is an informal meeting between two or more people. It's used internally for small meetings that don't fit into the 1:1 category (e.g. a manager meets someone who isn't one of their direct reports).

Chair	A nominated meeting attendee, who controls the meeting from start to finish. The chair coordinates the agenda, opens the meeting, and acts as facilitator. The chair will also sign off actions and minutes, before they are published.
Chatham House Rule	Under the 'Chatham House' rule, anyone who comes to a meeting is free to use information from the discussion, outside of the meeting. But they are not allowed to reveal who made a particular comment, or the name of the company that person is affiliated to. The rule is designed to promote openness of discussion, and to protect anonymity.
Committee	A group of people appointed within an organisation, to focus on a specific topic. Committee members work collaboratively, and make decisions as a group.
Conference	A conference is a large gathering of people, who come together to discuss a specific topic. Conferences usually have keynote speakers who are experts in their field, and deliver speeches to attendees. There are usually breakout sessions where attendees can choose to participate in smaller, more intimate, discussions on specific topics.
Conference Call	An audio, web based, or video call in which multiple participants join the same call, at the same time, using a meeting link or a bridge number. Calls are mostly via VoIP, and connect the users via an internet connection.
De-Brief	An internal meeting that takes place after a client or supplier meeting, to discuss what was successful and what wasn't. Internal actions are also agreed.
Delegate	A person representing others, or acting on behalf of another e.g. - A delegate at an event or conference, who is representing their organisation. - A calendar manager (delegate), granted delegate permissions by their manager.
EMEA	Europe, Middle East, and Africa (EMEA) is an acronym that global firms use, when dividing their operations by geography (or markets). It's an acronym that's widely used.
Face to Face	A meeting where attendees meet in-person.

Huddle	A daily meeting usually 5-15 mins in duration, to discuss tactical issues and provide updates.
In-Person	Attendees join the meeting in-person, not online or by audio call.
LATAM	Another label used by multinationals to describe a business region or market. LATAM is short for Latin America and the region is made up of South America, Mexico, Central America, and the islands of the Caribbean.
Minutes	Minutes of a meeting (the minutes) are an official summary of what happened during a meeting. Minutes are a record of objectives, decisions, and next steps. Minutes aren't a verbatim account of everything said, but are designed so that if someone who didn't attend the meeting read them later, they'd be able to understand what happened.
Mop-up	Similar to a de-brief. A meeting focusing on the end of a project or activity 'post event', to discuss its success, and to close the activity.
Month-End	A monthly meeting, to review the company's internal accounting and financial information.
NA	The region of countries making up North America.
QBR	A quarterly business review is a quarterly in-depth review, of the services provided to individual clients. Often involving cross functional collaboration and input.
Quarterly	In business terms a quarter refers to a 3 month period.
Quorum	The minimum number of attendees who have to be present for that meeting to proceed (for formal meetings e.g. boards or committees).
Recurring	Meetings that repeat regularly e.g. weekly, fortnightly, monthly.
Scrum	Term used in product development. A Scrum meeting can refer to any meeting, held by a Scrum agile team, during a product's development.
Seminar	A seminar is smaller than a conference, and it's typically focused on a single topic. Seminars involve a panel of experts who lead a discussion, and attendees have the opportunity to ask questions, and participate in the discussion.
Skip-Level Meeting	A skip-level meeting is simply a meeting where a manager meets with a direct report's team, on an individual basis,

	without that direct report in attendance. The direct report has been skipped. So a level 5 manager meets a level 3 employee, and skips their level 4 direct report.
SLT	The Senior Leadership Team, often referred to as SLT.
Stand-Up	A short meeting, often daily, for team members to share ideas on how to move the project forward quickly. Historically these meetings required attendees to come together and 'stand-up', instead of sitting around a conference table. Standing-up is less comfortable, but it gets people focused.
Summit	A conference or meeting, exclusively for executive level attendees. Often by invitation only.
Tentative	You 'may' be able to attend the meeting. Your attendance isn't confirmed, yet.
Town Hall	A meeting where everyone is invited. The business provides updates, and welcomes questions at the end. More recently called an 'All Hands'. Often held online for larger organisations, and recorded and shared afterwards for those who missed it, or were in a different time zone and unable to join live.
Virtual	Any meeting which is hosted online. Also known as webinars, video conferencing, web conferencing and online meetings.
Watercooler	Daily meetings where colleagues meet, and have informal catch-ups. The term came from real life habits, of people talking by the water cooler in the office, and exchanging ideas. The concept was soon adopted to online and virtual meetings.
Workshop	A group of people meeting for intense discussion, research or learning a specific topic. Usually a full day event with a structured agenda and presentations. Workshops are typically led by an expert, who demonstrates how to do something, or is invited to present on a topic they specialise in.

Collaborate with your exec by using the correct meeting terminology, consistently, when scheduling your bosses' meetings. For example, when you issue 1:1s have you used the exact same abbreviation for all directs? Or have you used a combination of 121, 1 on 1?

Whenever you issue a new meeting cadence, always agree the meeting title with your exec. Ensure it captures the meeting subject accurately, so attendees understand the purpose of the meeting at a glance. If your exec has suggested a meeting title that isn't clear, suggest a new one. Your input matters, because you're the calendar manager.

We've covered a lot of meeting expertise in this section. Now its time to put your knowledge into practice, and optimise the calendar...

6

Calendar Optimisation

STEP 34. What's a Calendar Audit?

If you've completed steps 31-33, you know what meeting cadence is, and you know the benefits of establishing meeting cadence in your exec's calendar. You've also familiarised yourself with meeting terminology and acronyms. As you're suitably equipped with the basics, you can move onto something more challenging in terms of delivery, and get your executive assistant teeth into a project.

You're going to start your very own project called '**Calendar Optimisation**'. The scope of the project is to:

- ✓ Analyse the content of your exec's calendar
- ✓ Challenge the effectiveness of current meeting cadence
- ✓ Collaborate with your executive and agree any changes
- ✓ Document and implement the changes

The goal is to create a highly optimised calendar for your executive, which contains strategically planned meetings. The new calendar will align with your executive's overall objectives, and have the correct meeting cadence throughout the year. This is hugely beneficial for your executive because you've helped them to focus on their priorities, eliminated the time stealers, and utilised their time more effectively.

The first stage of the project is to complete a **calendar audit,** and this will help you to establish which existing recurring meetings are relevant, which ones can be removed, and if any new meetings are required.

Imagine you've just landed a new job, and the calendar you've been given to manage is a mess. There are double bookings, overlaps, meeting churn and inconsistencies with meeting cadence. Where do you start? The best place to start is with a **calendar audit**.

During the **calendar audit**, you're going to examine the content of the calendar methodically, and assess its current condition, before discussing changes with your exec.

Lots of professionals complete 'audits', in order to assess whether something is working as effectively as it should, as well as looking for any errors. Financial audits are often completed in-house, by external auditors such as KPMG, PwC, Deloitte, EY, etc.

 An 'audit' is the term used to describe a methodical examination of a process, situation, or document, to determine its quality or condition.

Are you familiar with the auditors being on site for 1 week at a time, at your company headquarters? That's because it takes a team of auditors a huge chunk of time, to examine the company's accounts carefully, and methodically. Auditors are looking for errors, duplication, and inconsistences.

Similar to a financial audit, a calendar audit takes a forensic look at the calendar, but with the added benefits of challenging the current systems and protocols. A calendar audit is a mechanism for Improving the framework that's already in place, and aligning the content with your bosses' objectives, for the next 12 months.

Completing a calendar audit isn't something your exec will ask you to do, because it's generally not on their radar. However, this is something you should initiate, as an executive assistant, because you're a professional calendar manager. You know a badly managed calendar when you see one, and you know what a truly optimised calendar should look like. Your exec doesn't necessarily know this, so you must lead the way.

As a 'next level' EA, and a strategic business partner to your executive, YOU are going to take ownership of the 'calendar optimisation project'. You're going to create a meeting cadence spreadsheet, listing all of the recurring meetings in the calendar. You'll add specific column headings and sorting buttons, so the data can be sorted and analysed (I have a template to share with you, for this exercise).

The meeting cadence spreadsheet will become an efficient tool, allowing you to view, sort, and filter, the content from your exec's calendar. It will become a supercharged catalyst, that allows you to identify the time stealers, the low priorities, and the inconsistencies in the schedule. You'll also look at the number of attendees invited to recurring meetings, and consider if those numbers are justifiable. Some meetings have too many attendees invited, and that can be counterproductive.

When you present the information to your exec, the spreadsheet will contain all the data to allow your exec to quickly decide which existing recurring meetings are no longer required (and should be deleted), and which new meetings should be co-ordinated and scheduled, for the year ahead.

 The calendar optimisation project allows you (the EA and calendar manager), to analyse existing meeting cadence. To collaborate with your boss, and challenge existing meeting effectiveness, and to agree a new strategic meeting cadence, for the next 12 months.

If this sounds like a huge piece of work, it's worth thinking about what you're trying to achieve here. A calendar **without** the correct meeting cadence in place is disorganised, chaotic, reactive, and ineffective. A calendar **with** the correct meeting cadence, is the complete opposite. It will be organised, prioritised, and aligned with your exec's objectives.

The correct meeting cadence will also help your executive to be strategic with their time. **Time is the most valuable commodity for any executive in business, and time is the commodity that is most often wasted. You can never get back 'lost' time, but you can allocate your exec's time wisely.**

Owning and initiating this project, will demonstrate that you're proactive and a professional calendar manager, who is determined to eliminate any unnecessary meetings in the schedule. It shows that you want to improve your exec's time management, by challenging the existing structure of the calendar, and reducing large numbers of attendees wherever possible.

Your executive simply doesn't have time to make a forensic examination of their calendar, and decide what's working and what isn't working, in relation to their meetings. Sometimes executives can be a passenger in their own calendar, rather than the driver, and completing this project will prevent your executive from losing control.

Think of a calendar audit as a time management exercise. Every recurring meeting your exec owns will be scrutinised, evaluated, and challenged, during a dedicated meeting with your executive, which you're going to chair.

For example, you support the CTO of a software company. During the calendar audit, you've identified a meeting called 'Project Blue Cloud', with far too many attendees, in fact 18 solution architects have been invited and 18 have accepted. You should suggest to your CTO that you reduce the 18 solution architects to 10. That frees up 8 solution architects to work on other tasks and projects within the business, and the new format meeting will run more effectively, with a reduced number of attendees. There's no way that 18 solution architects are contributing to every single meeting, so make your boss aware of the numbers and suggest a reduction.

Imagine you support the SVP of business development in a management consultancy. The calendar audit has revealed a 2 x weekly, 1 hour meeting, focusing on 'Talent Acquisition' with the talent acquisition manager. That's 2 hours of your SVP's time, dedicated to talent acquisition every week. Do they really need 2 hours every week on this topic, when the meeting content could be condensed into a 1 hour weekly update meeting?

What's a Calendar Audit?

As the calendar manager, you should highlight this to your SVP, and agree a new format of 1 hour per week. That's reclaiming 1 hour of your exec's time, every week. That's a total of 4 hours every month which you've recovered, that can be re-purposed by your SVP, and they'll be super grateful for that.

Time is the most valuable commodity for any executive in business, and time is also the commodity that is most often wasted. You can never get back lost time, but you can allocate your executive's time wisely.

If, during the calendar audit, you spot a recurring meeting with a direct report who changed reporting lines, and is no longer a direct report of your exec, you can challenge the relevance of that meeting, and potentially cancel it. Because your exec should allocate their time to their own direct reports, not somebody else's.

Maybe there's a weekly meeting on 'Project Fusion', which you know has changed ownership from your exec to the COO, but it's still showing in the calendar on Thursdays for 2 hours. That should definitely be transferred to the COO, and removed from your exec's calendar.

In addition, completing a calendar audit, will prompt you to action calendar housekeeping tasks along the way, e.g. removing outdated meeting invites, declining irrelevant meetings, and deleting any time blockers which are no longer required.

Taking the initiative and completing a calendar audit will definitely get you brownie points, and you don't need your manager's consent to get started.

WARNING: if you haven't completed a calendar audit before, it's already long overdue. Block regular time in your calendar for 'Calendar Optimisation', and complete the steps within 5 working days. Use the checklist below, and follow steps 35-43 to complete the tasks.

Project: Calendar Optimisation

- ☐ Create a 'Meeting Cadence' spreadsheet

- ☐ Insert Column Headings

- ☐ Enter the data

- ☐ Add Filters

- ☐ Sort and Colour Code

- ☐ Meeting Prep (Calendar Analysis)

- ☐ Schedule a 'Calendar Audit' Meeting

- ☐ The Calendar Audit Meeting

- ☐ Attack to Win!

STEP 35. Create a 'Meeting Cadence' Spreadsheet

To improve your exec's time management, you need to analyse everything in the calendar, and ensure its accurate, relevant, and a priority for your exec. You're going to drop all the recurring meeting data into a spreadsheet called 'Meeting Cadence'. Then you're going to schedule time with your exec, to review the meeting data, line by line, together.

During the meeting, you'll challenge each line entry, and strategise for the next 12 months ahead. Finally, you'll implement the changes agreed. The process is called a calendar audit. The result is a fully optimised calendar, which aligns with your executive's objectives.

The first step in the process, is to build a spreadsheet for use during the calendar audit. When the spreadsheet is populated and formatted correctly, you're going to analyse and question the contents of all recurring meetings in the calendar. The frequency they're held, the number of attendees required, and whether the meeting duration is the right length. Then, together with your boss, you'll agree to make changes, (to elevate your executive from the meetings they don't need to attend, so that they can focus on the ones they do).

In Step no. 34 'What's a Calendar Audit', I explained why executive assistants should own the critical element of calendar optimisation, and why you don't have to wait to be asked to complete a calendar audit, by your line manager.

As an EA, you're responsible for both calendar management and calendar optimisation, and completing a calendar audit is integral to the success of operating a strategically driven calendar. Remember those financial auditors from KPMG, PwC, Deloitte, and EY? They regularly complete financial audits for companies, to ensure that everything is operating as smoothly as possible. You're going to do the same, but with your exec's calendar.

The calendar audit process described in this book; contains the exact same method I use, to examine the contents of a calendar for my executive. Whether I've just started in a new role, or just been allocated a new executive to support, the method is the same.

As a CEO level EA, employed on a contract basis, I change roles and companies, on average, every 9-12 months. Which means every 9-12 months I get a new calendar, or calendars, to manage.

Completing a calendar audit, at the beginning of a new EA contract, allows me to align with my exec on their strategy for the months ahead, and agree the correct meeting cadence required, in order to deliver their objectives. It also gives me the green light to remove any outdated meetings, decline any non-priority meetings, and ensure that the correct number of 1:1s are in place, for all of my exec's direct reports, for the remainder of the year.

Now it's your turn, and you're going to create a well-honed, meticulously crafted, and efficient calendar, which is optimised for performance. Let's break the project down into bite sized pieces, because breaking a project down into smaller steps is a proven project management technique, which can be adapted for busy calendar managers.

You'll never get a full day to work on a project like this, because of all the other things you must prioritise first, such as business travel, meeting support, event management etc. However, if you attack this in bite sized pieces, it becomes a manageable and easily achievable initiative.

Using the clipboard checklist in the previous step as your guide, your first task is to **create a Meeting Cadence spreadsheet** for the existing recurring meetings in the calendar. I should point out that if you're managing multiple calendars (for multiple execs) you'll need to complete this project separately for each exec. But once you've mastered the steps from beginning through to completion (for one exec), it will be a much quicker process the second time around.

There are a couple of ways to create a meeting cadence spreadsheet, showing all of your executive's recurring meetings. The first option is to export the data from Outlook or Google Calendar via the import/export function. You can google the exact steps for completing this, depending on the operating system you're running (Microsoft or Google Workspace) but you'll need to transfer the calendar data to a CSV file so you can work on it in excel or google sheets.

The second option is to manually populate your spreadsheet. This is my preferred option and I'll explain why, below.

Option 1: Export an Outlook calendar to Excel

This method does what it says on the tin (exports the calendar), but it doesn't provide a clear set of data to work with. Its time consuming to manipulate the data, and to remove any data you don't need. Outlook will export **all** calendar data and unfortunately it exports **everything**. You'll end up with a massive spreadsheet to sift through, which is unhelpful. Any recurring meetings will be listed individually by date, so you won't even see the cadence.

Open Outlook, open the calendar you want to export, click File / Open & Export / Import / Export / Export to a File / Next / Comma Separated Values / Next / Select Calendar to export from / Next / Browse / enter a file name and location (ensure CSV shows as file type) / Next / Set the dates for the export / Finish. Open the export from wherever you saved the file (or search for it by name if it's not obvious).

Option 2: Manually enter the Data into a Spreadsheet

The second option is to build a spreadsheet first, and then add the data manually. Whilst this is the 'manual' approach, it will save you time on sifting through any irrelevant data that will be exported automatically, using the import/export function in option 1.

Before you transfer the data into the spreadsheet, it's important to create the correct column headings, which will boost the calendar analysis. Take a look at the template on the next page.

When you're ready, move onto Step 36 and we'll do a deep dive into the spreadsheet template, and why you need to insert exactly the same column headings.

Meeting Cadence Spreadsheet Template

No.	Meeting Name	Category	Business Area	Attendees	Cadence	Day	Duration	Host	Updated 2023	Comment
1										
2										
3										
4										
5										
6										
7										
8										
9										
10										

STEP 36. Insert Column Headings

Before you host the 'calendar audit' meeting with your boss, you need to prepare well, and that preparation involves building a 'meeting cadence' spreadsheet. The spreadsheet will contain all the recuring meeting data from your exec's calendar. Each recurring meeting series will be split out into its individual components. There's 2 reasons for doing this:

1. Displaying the data in a spreadsheet makes analysis easier.
2. Presenting the data to your exec in this format is efficient. The data will be easy to read, and structured in a way that decisions can be made quickly.

An executive's time is invariably short on supply, so if you prepare well for the calendar audit meeting with your boss, you'll maximise the time you have during the meeting, and achieve the best output possible. In this instance, being well prepared equates to having a spreadsheet ready to go. Showing all the recurring meetings your exec has in their calendar at that moment, split out by the following column headings:

A.	Number	G.	Day
B.	Meeting Name	H.	Duration
C.	Category	I.	Host
D.	Business Area	J.	Updated
E.	Attendees	K.	Comments
F.	Cadence		

Spending time on preparing the spreadsheet, before your calendar audit meeting, will accelerate your meeting progress. It will enhance collaboration when viewing the spreadsheet together, and enable you to update the spreadsheet with actions, along the way.

Displaying the data in an easily viewable and structured spreadsheet, versus viewing the calendar together 'live', will enable your exec to hone-in on the recurring meetings, analyse the meeting components, and make strategic decisions quickly, during your meeting. It will assist your exec to clearly identify which meetings can stay, and which meetings can go.

 Presenting the data in this format, will make your calendar audit meeting run so efficiently, that you'll be able to complete it with your boss in 30 mins. Yes, seriously! A whole calendar reviewed, analysed and actions agreed in 30 mins, when using this format.

When I completed this exercise in December 2022, for the CEO I was supporting in a fintech start-up, he had 33 recurring meetings in his calendar. That's 33 meetings that repeated regularly, all year round. It didn't include all the other meetings in his calendar, such as client meetings, investor meetings, or candidate interviews, which fell into the 'one off' or 'ad hoc' meeting category.

Let's look at each column heading in more detail, and why you need them. Using the template as your guide, you need a *'Number' column (A)* on the left hand side, to capture the number of recurring meetings that are currently in the calendar. You may be surprised at the total number of meetings present.

	A	B	C	D
1	No.	Meeting Name ⌄	Category ⌄	Business Area ⌄
2	1			
3	2			
4	3			

Meeting Name (B) This should be the exact name of the meeting as it appears in the calendar.

Category (C) Allocate categories to each of your exec's meetings. This will allow you to sort all the meetings into categories BEFORE you share the data with your exec. Here is an example of the categories I created for my CEO's calendar audit:

Executive	***Direct Report***	***Team***
External	***Indirect Report***	***Coach***

You'll need to create categories relevant to your own executive's meetings, but you can use my examples as a starting point. The key is to identify the different types of meetings, that fall in the calendar. Allocate a name to each type of meeting (a category), so that you can group them together, using the filter tools. Below are the categories I used, and the criteria I used to categorise each meeting. View the table and decide which categories work best for you.

Category Name	Type of meeting
Executive	Internal meetings of the highest priority and meetings with the most senior stakeholders e.g. Chairperson, Senior Leadership Team, Executive Committee, QBR, Board Meeting, Advisory Board, Month-End.
External	Clients, Investors, Suppliers, meetings where the attendees are external to the company.
Direct Report	Any of your exec's direct reports (employees they manage).
Indirect report	Not a direct report but likely to be a sync or catch-up on a 1:1 basis.
Team	Internal meeting with 3+ attendees (not a 1:1).
Coach	Your exec may have an executive coach or business coach. This has its own category, as its not strictly work focused, more leadership development.

The categories you allocate, will help you to filter and sort the data in the spreadsheet (more on that later).

Business Area (D) is for the business function, or department name, of the meeting's focus. This will allow you to sort meetings by their business area, and allow you to see where your exec's time is spent the most. I used the following labels for my CEO's business areas:

> **Business Development**
>
> **Executive Assistant**
>
> **Finance**
>
> **Growth**
>
> **Human Resources**
>
> **Leadership Team**
>
> **Legal**
>
> **Operations**
>
> **Personal Development**
>
> **Product**

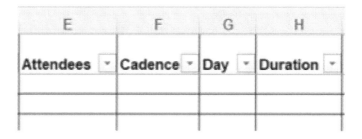

Attendees (E) To capture the number of attendees, who are joining your exec at the meeting. For instance: for 1:1s, input 1 (as its 1 person meeting your executive). This makes all 1:1s clearly visible in the spreadsheet, as they're numbered 1 in the column.

Column E (Attendees) will prove hugely impactful, because you'll identify the meetings with high volumes of attendees quickly. Meetings that have a large number of attendees should be challenged. Depending on the focus of the meeting, having a large number of attendees may be counterproductive. This is why using the appropriate column headings are advantageous to the audit.

You're stripping back meetings to their individual components, and analysing each individual component of that meeting. And that's just not possible if you try to complete a calendar audit, by looking at the calendar 'live' with your boss, during a 30 minute meeting.

When I completed my last calendar audit, I identified a 'Weekly Sales & Marketing Meeting', that had 38 attendees for 90 mins duration. That's a lot of attendees! That's just not a productive use of 38 peoples' time, because there's no way 38 people are going to contribute during that meeting. During the audit meeting with my boss, I discovered that over a period of time, the sales and marketing team numbers had swelled, as the start-up had grown in size. But the meeting cadence had remained the same.

What needed to happen (and the calendar audit process triggered this) was for the 2 teams (Sales and Marketing) to be split out by business area, and have their own individual team meetings. The total number of 38 would become 2 smaller meetings of 20 and 18. The smaller meetings would enable increased focus, better collaboration, and groups sizes where everyone could participate. The duration for each new meeting would be 60 minutes.

During the calendar audit meeting I had with my boss, I suggested this course of action, and we agreed that the meeting cadence should change. I deleted the original 'Weekly Sales and Marketing' series, and created a new series for the 'Sales Team' and a separate series for the 'Marketing Team'.

Cadence (F) This column will capture the meeting frequency e.g. weekly, fortnightly, every 6 weeks, monthly, quarterly etc.

Day (G) The day of the week the meeting lands on. This is useful because if you see several meetings all landing on the same day e.g. Mondays, you might prefer to spread them out evenly across the week. Or, if too many meetings are landing on Wednesdays, you can move some over to a quieter day. Abbreviate the days in the column to their first 3 letters e.g. Mon, Tue, Wed.

Duration (H) The length of the meeting in minutes, or hours (if 2 hours or more).

Host (I) Whose meeting is it? If your exec is the meeting organiser, add their name here. You can move or amend the meeting, with your exec's permission. If someone else organises the meeting, add their name in this column. You'll need to approach them, or their EA, with any change requests.

Updated (J) When you build your spreadsheet, leave the cells in this column blank. As you work on each action agreed by your boss, input the date here, to show when you completed it.

Comment (K) This is for any comments you may want to add, for each line entry, BEFORE you share this with your exec. You can add your own observations here, as a reminder of the points to raise during the meeting. Such as, "Is this meeting still required?" or "Do you need this weekly?" or "Can we amend this to fortnightly?"

Space the columns out evenly and bold the headings. Ctrl + B is the bold shortcut. When you've inserted the column headings, you're ready to start populating your spreadsheet. Move onto Step 37, and 'Enter the Data using Advanced Search'.

STEP 37. Enter the Data using 'Advanced Search'

With the column headings in place, it's time to add the details of all of your exec's recurring meetings, into the spreadsheet. As explained in Step 35, you can either use the 'calendar export' function to automate the export, or you can type the data in manually. If you're going to use the 'calendar export' function, remember to delete the 'non-recurring' meetings that will be included in the export, because they aren't relevant to the calendar audit.

For the manual method, there is a hack to help you locate the recurring meetings quickly, so you don't have to scan the calendar yourself. There is a feature in Outlook Calendar called **'Advanced Search'**, you just need to know where to find it.

'Advanced Search' will save you time, and prevent you from having to manually look for the recurring meetings. Using the advanced search function ensures that you capture ALL the recurring meetings in your exec's calendar, and won't miss any.

Manually searching for recurring meetings in your exec's calendar, isn't as time consuming as you might think, because there's a tool in Outlook (and Google Calendar) that does this for you. **Advanced Search** will allow you to search for all recurring meetings, and show them in a 'list' view.

Follow the steps below, to complete a search for all recurring meetings in your exec's calendar. Then, input the results into your 'meeting cadence' spreadsheet.

Using the 'Advanced Search' Function in Outlook

Open the Outlook Calendar you want to run the recurring meeting search in. Close any other calendar folders.

Enter the Data using 'Advanced Search'

Go to the very top of your screen. Place your cursor in the search bar.

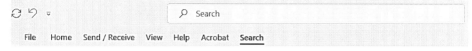

On the left hand side, select the drop down arrow next to 'All Calendar Items' and select 'Current Folder'.

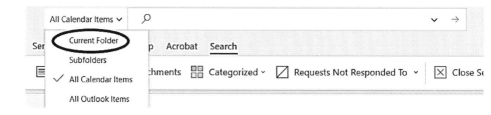

Select the drop down arrow on the right.

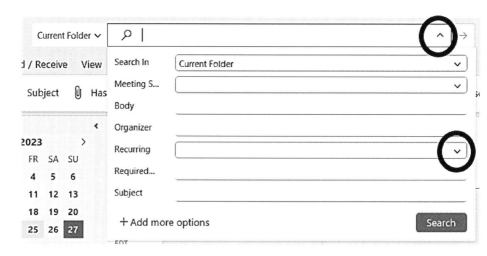

By the 'Recurring' field, select the drop down arrow, and select Yes. Select Search.

The **Advanced Search** function will generate a list of all the recurring meetings in the calendar.

Results

🗋	📎	Subject	Location	Start
v Daily: 2 item(s)				
📅		Product Update		Thu 13/07/2023 09:30
📅		Time to learn!		Tue 11/07/2023 17:00
v Weekly: 2 item(s)				
📅		Liam 1on1		Wed 12/07/2023 14:00
📅		Weekly Leadership Team Meting		Tue 11/07/2023 11:00
v Monthly: 4 item(s)				
📅	📎	TC-EAA Monthly Lunch Meeting	https://us02web.zoo...	Thu 10/09/2020 18:00
📅	📎	CEAA Monthly Lunch Meeting	https://us02web.zoo...	Thu 12/11/2020 18:00

And will group them by their **recurrence pattern** (their cadence).

Recurrence Pattern
every day from 17:00 to 17:30
every weekday from 09:30 to 10:00
every Tuesday from 11:00 to 13:00
every Wednesday from 14:00 to 15:00
the second Thursday of every 1 month(s) from 12:00 to 13:00

From the results view, you can double click on each entry to open them in a second window. Using the search results as your guide, extract the recurring meeting data you need, and insert it into your meeting cadence spreadsheet.

When you've populated the spreadsheet with all of your exec's recurring meetings, move on to Step 38 and 'add filters'.

STEP 38. Add Filters

Your meeting cadence spreadsheet should now include all of your exec's recurring meetings, line by line.

The next action required is to **add filters** to your column headings. Adding filter buttons will allow you to display only the data you need, based on certain criteria. The data you don't need to see, can be hidden temporarily from view.

For example, you can filter by 'Cadence' to show 'weekly' meetings only, you can filter data by 'Duration' to show only the '30 min' meetings, and you can filter by 'Business Area' to view the 'Leadership Team' meetings.

Being able to filter the recurring meeting data, is invaluable when you complete analysis of the spreadsheet (Step 40). There are 3 ways to do this:

3 ways to add filter in Excel

1. On the Data tab, in the Sort & Filter group, click the Filter button.
2. On the Home tab, in the Editing group, click Sort & Filter > Filter.
3. Use the Excel Filter shortcut to turn the filters on/off: Ctrl+Shift+L.

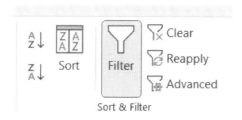

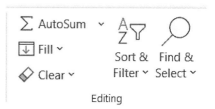

With the filter buttons in place, you can manipulate the data by selecting the filter dropdown, uncheck **Select All**, and select the specific data you want to see.

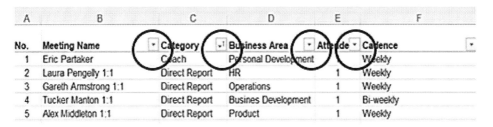

Play around with the filter functionality, for each column heading in your spreadsheet. You can apply more than 1 filter at once. To clear filters, go back to the filter tool options and select 'clear'.

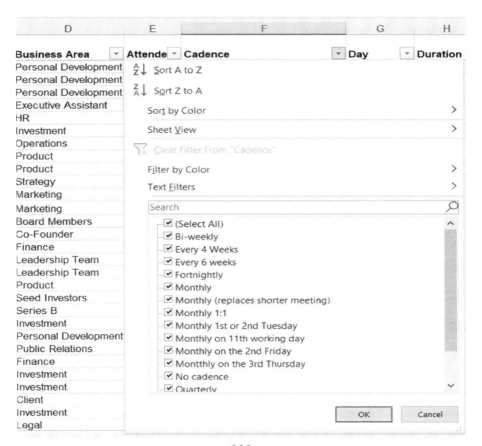

STEP 39. Sort and Colour Code

You're halfway through the 'Calendar Optimisation Project', and the majority of the groundwork is complete. You've created and populated a 'meeting cadence spreadsheet' with the relevant column headings. All your exec's recurring meetings are listed, and split out to show their individual components.

You've added filter buttons, and you can filter the data by meeting name, category, business area, attendee numbers, cadence and so on. There's a couple more tools to utilise within excel, so you can manage and present the data in the best format possible.

Firstly, you can **sort** your data by using the A-Z (ascending order), and Z-A (descending order) tools.

To locate the Sort A-Z buttons, click on the filter button, next to the category you want to sort. Select the type of sort you want to complete.

When I completed this task, I sorted by A-Z by Category. I checked the box Select All, and used the Sort A to Z function.

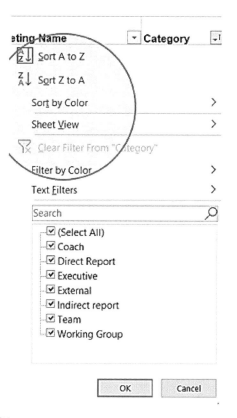

The results (image below) show Category Column C, sorted in alphabetical order, from Direct Report to Team. This is the format I used, when presenting the data to my CEO.

Secondly, if you want to get really fancy, you can **colour code** the categories, which will add another visible dimension. By adding colours you can utilise another filter option in the spreadsheet 'sort by colour'.

Once you've coloured the cells, Excel allows you to **sort and filter** by cell colours. Use the highlight and fill colour icon, to colour cells.

For instance, you could colour code all executive level meetings red. Next, use the **filter by colour** tool and select red. Only the executive level meetings will display.

By choosing the **sort by colour** tool and choosing red, you can re-order the data, starting with red.

Rather than allocating a rainbow of colours to your spreadsheet, to make it look pretty, think about using a colour for priority meetings only. Colours are a nice touch, but don't make the spreadsheet look too busy, by using every colour in the rainbow. It's the data that matters, not the colours. Another method is to use one colour palette e.g. red, and use dark red to illustrate the high priority meetings, and the palest red for the low priority meetings, such as 1:1s etc.

Now you can sort, colour code, and display the data in many ways, which will enable you to have a really productive meeting with the calendar owner (your exec). Your finished spreadsheet should look similar to the one on the next page. The next step is to analyse the data, and prepare for the calendar audit meeting.

Meeting Cadence Spreadsheet with sample data

No.	Meeting Name	Category	Business Area	Attende	Cadence	Day	Duration	Host
1	Eric Partaker	Coach	Personal Development	1	Weekly	Tue	75 mins	Brad
2	Laura Pengelly 1:1	Direct Report	HR	1	Weekly	Wed	30 mins	Brad
3	Gareth Armstrong 1:1	Direct Report	Operations	1	Weekly	Wed	30 mins	Brad
4	Tucker Manton 1:1	Direct Report	Busines Development	1	Bi-weekly	Tue, Fri	30 mins	Brad
5	Alex Middleton 1:1	Direct Report	Product	1	Weekly	Tue	30 mins	Brad
6	Kurian Bhagat 1:1	Direct Report	IT	1	Weekly	Mon	30 mins	Brad
7	Board Meeting	Executive	Board Members	7	Every 6 weeks	Wed or Thu	3 hours	Brad
8	Review Month-End Results	Executive	Finance	2	Monthly on 11th working day	Various	60 mins	Michelle
9	Product Executive Board	Executive	Product	8	Monthly 1st or 2nd Tuesday	Tue	2 hours	Dimple
10	Richard James	Executive	Co-Founder	1	Weekly	Thu	60 mins	Brad
11	Series B	Executive	Growth	5	Weekly	Mon	30 mins	Kristin
12	Senior Leadership Team	Executive	Leadership Team	8	Weekly	Mon	2 hours	Brad
13	YPO Forum	External	Personal Development	10	Monthly on the 3rd Thursday	Thu	3 hours	Lokendra
14	Advisory Board Update	External	Growth	124	Quarterly	Fri	60 mins	Krupali
15	Felix Gooch Catch-Up	Indirect report	Finance	1	Bi-weekly	Fri	30 mins	Brad
16	Legal & Compliance SteerCo	Team	Legal	5	Fortnightly	Tue	30 mins	Liam
17	Biz Dev Weekly Sync	Team	Busines Development	10	Weekly	Mon	60 mins	Tucker

STEP 40. Meeting Prep (Spreadsheet Analysis)

Before you complete the calendar audit meeting with your exec, have a really good look at the meeting cadence spreadsheet you've created. Analyse the content. Study the spreadsheet in detail, line by line. Work your way through the data from left to right. Look closely at the components of each meeting. Spend time on analysing the content by category, meeting name, and business area.

 'Analysis is a detailed examination of anything complex, in order to understand its nature, or to determine its essential features' *(Merriam-Webster)*. Completing a careful analysis of the meeting cadence spreadsheet, is an essential element of the audit process.

The last time I completed this exercise for a CEO, I noticed multiple things from viewing the spreadsheet, that I hadn't noticed from viewing his calendar, and I was working on that particular calendar every day.   The inconsistencies, the errors, the time stealers, and the overpopulated meetings, literally jumped out at me, when I analysed the spreadsheet.

As a result of analysing the meeting cadence spreadsheet for that particular CEO (of a tech start-up), I identified 12 issues with his calendar. For each one, I listed what I'd identified, and the question I wanted to ask him, during our calendar audit meeting. Let's take a look at what I identified, and how I was going to raise the issues with my boss:

My Spreadsheet Analysis: Observations and Comments

1   Only 6 (out of 10) of your direct reports have regular 1:1s with you. Should I schedule the 1:1s that are missing?

2   Some of your 1:1s are recurring weekly, some are bi-weekly, is that correct?

3   Your 1:1s are all 60 mins duration, could they be reduced to 30 mins?

4   Senior Leadership Team meeting: only has 5 attendees, is that correct? *(Out of a potential 7 I'd identified)*

5   Your Executive Coaching sessions: 1 coach has a weekly cadence, 1 has fortnightly, 1 has no cadence, is that correct? *(The CEO I was supporting had 3 different coaches).*

6   Board Meetings *(with external attendees)* are recurring every month, should we push back to every 6 or 8 weeks?

7   Nadir Javid, has monthly 1:1s with you, but is an 'indirect' report, is this still required?

8   Advisory Boards: showing as 4 weeks cadence, is that too often?

9   Weekly Sales & Marketing meeting: has 38 attendees, is that too many?

10   Should the Sales & Marketing meeting be split out into 2 separate meetings e.g. 1. Sales Team and 2. Marketing Team?

11   Operations Team meeting: this is a 'team' call, do you need to join? *(CEOs don't usually join 'team' meetings due to their seniority. I didn't feel the Ops Team meeting was a priority, or a good use of his time, so I challenged it).*

12   You join a total of 6 team meetings. Which ones are relevant? Which ones can I decline?

After I'd completed the analysis, I visited **Comments Column K** of the master spreadsheet, and inserted my observations and comments, exactly as they are shown here.

Completing the analysis prior to the audit meeting, enabled me to raise the issues quickly, during the meeting. I was able to work through the points, line by line. Having a written record also kept me 'on point' during our meeting. Whenever our meeting veered off in another direction, I got it back on track, and covered the queries I wanted to discuss. I used the comments column like my own written agenda.

Prepare for your calendar audit meeting with your boss, by analysing the meeting cadence spreadsheet thoroughly. Use the sort and filter buttons to cross check the data. Record your findings, with proposed solutions, in the Comment's column.

Use the following prompts, to complete your spreadsheet analysis:

> **?** What patterns do you see?
> **?** What inconsistencies do you notice?
> **?** Are there meetings your exec doesn't need to join?
> **?** Are there meetings lasting 2 hours or more that could be reduced?
> **?** Is Monday a heavy meeting day?
> **?** Can you see meetings with far too many attendees?
> **?** Are there any duplications?
> **?** What else jumps out at you?

 Add your observations and proposed solutions in the Comments column. Use them as prompts to refer to, when you complete the calendar audit meeting with your boss.

The 3 x Meeting Rules of Elon Musk

South African-born American entrepreneur, and businessman, Elon Musk, shared his own thoughts on meetings, with his employees back in 2018. He sent an email to Tesla employees that outlined, amongst other things, 3 clear meeting rules to follow:

1. Please get rid of all large meetings, unless you're certain they are providing value to the whole audience, in which case keep them very short.

2. Get rid of frequent meetings unless you are dealing with an extremely urgent matter. Meeting frequency should drop rapidly once the urgent matter is resolved.

3. Walk out of a meeting or drop off a call as soon as it's obvious you aren't adding value. It's not rude to leave, it's rude to make someone stay and waste their time.

Elon Musk is one of the richest people in the World. He's the CEO of multiple businesses and he regularly challenges process and procedure. Whatever you think of him as a personality or employer, he does have a point with his 3 x Meeting Rules.

Personally, I've seen so many calendars where executives are back to back in meetings, all day, every day, that they don't have time to draw breath. On the surface this may 'look' productive, but you have to ask yourself is it really necessary? Is it 'really' productive? And is it a good use of your executive's time?

Challenging bad calendar habits is definitely in scope for an EA, you just need to be diplomatic when doing it.

Spending time on spreadsheet analysis, before the calendar audit meeting with your exec, will allow you to be prepared, and to dive straight in on the inconsistencies, the overpopulated meetings, or any meetings which are unnecessary for your exec to join.

Potentially, you've only got a 30 minute window, to complete a calendar audit with your busy exec. So do the meeting prep, and record your observations with proposed solutions, ahead of time. Completing meeting prep beforehand, puts you firmly in the driving seat when the meeting starts, and it's going to give you confidence to tackle the issues you've identified head on.

Analysing the spreadsheet, prior to the meeting with your exec, is critical to the success of the calendar audit, and the output you'll agree with your exec. When you've completed your analysis, and inserted comments into column K, move onto the next step.

STEP 41. Schedule a 'Calendar Audit' Meeting

You've already completed steps 34-40, of the calendar optimisation project. That's a sizeable piece of work done and out the way – fantastic! The next step is to schedule a 'calendar audit' meeting with your boss (the calendar owner), so you can collaborate and complete a calendar audit together.

You may think to yourself, "Do I really need to schedule a calendar audit meeting with my exec? Couldn't I just email the spreadsheet over to them instead?" If you go down that route *(and believe me it's tempting as we don't like to challenge our executives, or take up more of their time than is necessary)*, you'll make very little progress, or may not even get a response.

If you email the meeting cadence spreadsheet to your exec, they'll categorise it as an 'admin' task, and put it to the back of the queue, together with their expenses, and any other admin things they don't want to do. They won't prioritise an email with a spreadsheet (about a calendar audit), because they won't understand what's required of them, or why.

At first glance it's just an Excel file with their meetings listed, together with column headings, sorting buttons and filters. You haven't explained the analysis you've completed, or the benefits of completing a calendar audit to them. At this stage you haven't piqued their interest, or secured their buy-in.

Because of the importance of completing a calendar audit, you must get dedicated meeting time booked in with your exec, to drive the project forward. You're an EA, and calendar management is what you do professionally, so this is a chance for you to step up and showcase your skills. Take the initiative, and request a dedicated meeting on this topic with your boss.

At the moment your boss probably doesn't even know what a calendar audit is, and why would they? This is your territory; it's your area of expertise, so take the lead and schedule a meeting, to focus them on this topic. Drive the overall project, through to completion.

You're going to request a **calendar audit meeting** with your exec, explain the objectives of the meeting, and steer them through the process. You'll record all actions agreed during the meeting, and then you'll implement them.

Position this the right way, and you'll get your manager's buy-in and adoption. Ultimately, you're doing them a big favour here, because you're going to improve their time management, and align their meetings with their objectives, for the forthcoming year.

A high proportion of executives don't take a step back from their calendars, to view what's going on in detail. They simply don't have time. But when you think about it, the calendar is the biggest productivity tool at their disposal, so it must work to their advantage.

Utilise the calendar well, and your executive's productivity will go through the roof. But if you fail to complete a calendar audit, your executive will be stuck in a constant loop of meetings, which are potentially unnecessary, too long in duration, with too many people (or the wrong people), and have the incorrect cadence. In other words – a total disaster and a complete waste of their time.

 Completing a calendar audit for your exec, not only challenges their recurring meetings, it's also a fantastic time management exercise. You're taking the initiative to help them evaluate where their time is being spent, and whether it's being spent wisely. You're questioning the effectiveness of each recurring meeting, and you're challenging the allocation of their time.

Don't feel nervous about embarking on this stage of the project. Whether you have a good relationship with your boss or not (and I hope you do) this is part of your responsibility as an executive assistant, and you're demonstrating that you have a **continuous improvement mindset**. Afterall, you're going to be doing all the work; you just need meeting time with your exec, and their input, before you can get stuck in.

Next time you have a 1:1 or catch-up call with your exec, explain that you're going to schedule a calendar audit meeting, for the 2 of you. Explain that you want to review the recurring meetings in the calendar, and that you've prepared a spreadsheet for sharing. Say that you'll pop the meeting time in, when you see an appropriate 30 minute gap.

That's it – that's all you need to share for now. When your exec sees the calendar entry, they'll know what it is. Look for a slot in their calendar, that you know is going to be a suitable time for the meeting. My suggestion is at the end of the week, and avoid a travel day. A work from home day is good, early morning is also good. You could even convert one of your usual 1:1s for this purpose.

Link the meeting cadence spreadsheet to the body of the meeting invite, so you can access it quickly during the meeting. Then, you're good to go!

STEP 42. The Calendar Audit Meeting

Get ready for the calendar audit meeting with your boss. Have the 'meeting cadence spreadsheet' open on your screen, ready to share when the meeting starts.

Ensure you've pre-sorted the data by **category**. This is how I sorted the data for the calendar audit meeting, with my CEO. Sorting by 'category' allows you to view similar meeting types together, e.g. direct reports, executive meetings, and external meetings.

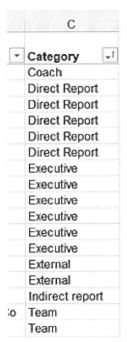

Grouping similar types of meetings together, so you can discuss and action them as 'one', is a technique known as **batching.** Batching involves grouping several individual data points into a 'mini batch' and dealing with them collectively, instead of dealing with them one by one. It's an effective way of tackling large amounts of data quickly. Batching makes the audit process more efficient, and more productive.

Another reason to sort the data by meeting category, is to improve the flow of the meeting with your boss. Imagine if your data hasn't been sorted, and row 1 of your spreadsheet shows a 1:1 meeting for a direct report. You discuss it with your exec, record the action agreed, and move onto the next row. The next row is an external meeting, you discuss it, and record the action. On the next row is a team meeting, and below that is an executive level meeting.

Can you see how you're shifting your exec's focus by doing it that way? Switching from one type of meeting category to another is ineffective, because your interrupting the flow of the decision making process. Jumping around from a direct report's 1:1, to an external meeting, to a team meeting, to an executive meeting, is confusing and its continually switching your exec's focus. However, if you complete the audit by batching the meeting types together (by category), it will keep your exec focused, speed up the decision making process, and achieve consistency. Try to discuss all the direct reports 1:1s together, then the exec levels, then the externals, then the team meetings.

When the calendar audit meeting commences, start by explaining the purpose and objective of the meeting. Use the following script as a guide:

"Thanks for your time today, we're going to complete an audit of the recurring meetings in your calendar, and ensure that they are relevant, with the right cadence, and the correct attendees. This is an opportunity for us to challenge the relevance of your recurring meetings, and determine what's working, what isn't working, and which changes are required.

I've completed my own analysis of your calendar, and I've prepared a spreadsheet showing all your recurring meetings, which I'll share with you now. I thought we could work through it together. I'll record any changes we agree in the spreadsheet, and I'll implement the changes for you.

The goal of the calendar audit is to identify any meetings which are no longer required, to free up some of your time, and allow you to be more strategic going forwards. Let's look at line 1 together... "

Read out the meeting on line 1, and refer to the comment's column. Prompt your executive with any challenging questions you've prepared, e.g. "can I reduce this from 1 hour to 30 mins?" or, "does this meeting need 28 attendees?" or, "is this meeting still required?".

The critical thing here is to **challenge** your exec during the calendar audit meeting, and keep them focused on completing the audit line by line. Rather than letting them skip ahead to the most senior level meetings, or the meetings with the longer durations.

If they do that (and its likely, because they are experienced enough to home in on the big ticket items), pull them back to the line you want to discuss. Say "can we come back to that one later?" Work through the data methodically with your exec, and don't skip to the big ticket items.

Here are some example **challenge questions** to ask your executive, during the calendar audit meeting:

Questions to challenge your exec's
'Bad Meeting Habits'

Q. How long should your 1:1s be?

Q. How frequent should your 1:1s be?

Q. Is the [blank] meeting series too frequent or not frequent enough?

Q. Does holding the [blank] meeting on Mondays work for you, or should it be later in the week?

Q. Can I reduce the [blank] meeting duration from 60 mins to 30 mins?

Q. Does the [blank] meeting need to be weekly, or can I adjust it to fortnightly?

Q. Does the [blank] meeting need 25 attendees *(or any big number you spot),* or can I reduce it?

Q. You have 3 calls a week with [blank], do you need that many?

Q. Which meetings can you delegate?

Q. Which meetings can you decline?

Q. Are you the correct owner of the [blank] meeting or should it move over to [blank]?

Q. Should I avoid scheduling anything before 09:00?

Q. Should I avoid scheduling across lunchtime?

Q. Should I avoid scheduling anything after 17:00?

Q. Are the right attendees invited to [blank]?

Q. Is the [blank] meeting still relevant?

Q. Which meetings are you spending too much time on?

Q. What do you need to spend more of your time on?

Q. Is the [blank] meeting in-person or online?

 Working on this with your exec, promotes collaboration when completing a calendar audit. The 'challenge questions' will support you through the meeting, and keep your manager focused. Using the challenge questions will also prompt your exec to be strategic, about the allocation of their time.

Insert a new column heading in your spreadsheet named 'Actions Agreed'. Use it to record the changes agreed with your boss. Capture the actions accurately, live, during the meeting. Do this right, the first time around. If an action is unclear, ask your exec to clarify it, before recording the action in the spreadsheet.

 Your objectives for the calendar audit meeting are: to challenge your exec on the current meeting cadence, flag the unnecessary meetings, question lengthy meeting durations, and reduce high volumes of attendees, wherever possible. By challenging the existing framework of the calendar, and agreeing a new improved cadence, you're enabling continuous improvement and making a big impact for your exec.

If you don't get to the end of your spreadsheet in one go, and run out of time, schedule another 30 min call to complete it with your boss, but do that ASAP.

STEP 43. Attack the Calendar

Now that the calendar audit meeting is over, you can congratulate yourself on your progress. You asked challenging questions, which prompted your exec to think strategically about the meetings they regularly host, and join. You created an **Actions Agreed** column in the meeting cadence spreadsheet, which shows all the changes you discussed with your exec.

You've demonstrated that you're pro-active and focused, with meticulous attention to detail. But above all, you've shown your boss that you're a professional calendar manager, with a continuous improvement mindset.

Well done! The hardest part (challenging your exec) is over, and it's pretty much plain sailing from now on.

 If you didn't manage to get through all the recurring meetings, during the time allocated with your boss, make sure you book a follow up session ASAP. Secure the time in the calendar today, whilst this is still front of mind.

When I completed this step of the calendar optimisation project, with my CEO, he agreed to a considerable amount of changes, and the challenge questions definitely made a big difference. Here's a summary of what happened, during my calendar audit meeting, with my CEO:

- ✓ He agreed to all of his 1:1s moving to a 30 minute duration (thereby achieving consistency across all direct reports).
- ✓ We moved the Board Meetings from a 4 week cadence to an 8 week cadence.
- ✓ We agreed that Advisory Boards would change cadence from every 4 weeks to once a quarter.
- ✓ We agreed to cancel the Sales & Marketing meeting series, and replace with 2 separate focused meetings, with smaller attendee numbers.

- ✓ A skip level direct report meeting was cancelled, as it was no longer required.
- ✓ A new Finance Review meeting was agreed, because the team had changed, and a new cadence was required.
- ✓ 2 team meetings were declined.
- ✓ 2 executive coaching meetings were confirmed as recurring fortnightly.
- ✓ 1 executive coaching meeting was no longer required, and the series was cancelled.
- ✓ There were several other small tweaks agreed, such as 'moving to Wednesdays', 'avoid after 17:00', and 'delegate that to [blank]'.

The calendar audit meeting with my exec was extremely productive, and time well spent. My CEO had never seen all of his meetings disseminated in a spreadsheet before, and he was eager to remove the meetings no longer required. But he did add in a couple of new ones!

After the meeting with your exec, the actions agreed will enable you to progress to the final step of the calendar optimisation project – the implementation. You've agreed a new meeting structure with your executive for the next 12 months, and now it's time to implement the changes.

It's time to ATTACK THE CALENDAR!

Attack the changes agreed, firstly by blocking time out in your own calendar to focus on this task. Don't do this critical step a disservice, by fitting it in when you can. Block 1-2 hours to **Attack the Calendar**. It's very important to action the changes agreed ASAP, in fact as soon as you've had the meeting with your boss, you should implement the changes within 24 hours.

Secondly, attention to detail is key, so don't multi-task, **single task**. Focus your attention on completing this task in one hit, and see it through to completion. Don't get distracted by emails, Slack, WhatsApp or whatever else is pinging notifications at you – ignore them. Calendar management must be accurate, don't invite the risk of errors into the process, by switching tasks or getting distracted.

When the calendar audit is complete, implement the changes agreed with your boss. Action all the changes ASAP, and set yourself a deadline of 24 hours to complete everything you've agreed.

If your executive asked you to wait, before initiating any of the changes, then you need to observe that request and wait. Add a reminder to your calendar to complete it later. Otherwise, you can continue to work through the spreadsheet and the actions agreed. As you work through the changes, update Column J 'Updated' with today's date, to identify that you've actioned the changes required for that meeting.

If you're removing meetings which are no-long required, that's a bonus because it will give you space in the calendar. When you issue a cancellation notification (to the meeting attendees), add a note confirming that the 'meeting is no longer required', so they understand the reason for the cancellation.

Continue working through the spreadsheet until you're done.

When you've implemented all the 'actions' recorded in your spreadsheet, you've reached the end of the **Calendar Optimisation Project**. Congratulations! You're a calendar audit winner! With the project complete, your exec's calendar will be in much better shape. It's been analysed, strategised, attacked, and optimised for performance – all thanks to you!

Next time you have a 1:1 with your boss, tell him or her that all the actions agreed during the audit meeting have been implemented, and that their calendar is optimised and ready to go!

When you dramatically improve upon something the first time around, the impact can be huge (like the calendar audit). But over time, things change. Meetings get added, invites are accepted, and more people join team meetings. Which is why you should repeat the calendar audit process 4 times a year (every quarter).

The first time (you complete a calendar audit) is going to take the most time, because you're building the spreadsheet from nothing, but from then on it gets much easier, and quicker, to repeat the process.

Add reminders to your calendar, to complete calendar audits for your executive, on a quarterly basis. Regular audits are a way of continuously improving your exec's calendar, and their time management. Next time you repeat the audit, create a copy of the original sheet, and rename it with the name of the quarter you're in. This allows you to keep a record of all the changes you make, over a 12 month period.

WARNING! I've shared the way I complete a calendar audit with you, using Excel / Google Sheets, and it's a comprehensive way of completing an audit for a company executive. A word of warning: if you choose to complete a calendar audit using calendar productivity apps beware! **External apps may pose a security risk**, and they won't be anywhere near as comprehensive as my tried and tested EA mastery method.

There are calendar productivity apps in existence which require permission to access your exec's calendar, to enable analytics and reporting. But be very cautious about giving your consent. Your basically sharing confidential information with a third party via the app, and that could have serious consequences for you (and your executive). You could also find yourself in breach of a company security or compliance policy. Always check with your IT department before downloading a calendar app, which isn't already installed on your device.

Congratulations on completing the calendar audit, and for challenging your boss on any of their bad meeting habits! Following the steps in the audit process will also give you confidence to complete it again, because you've seen the results it delivers to your executive. Remember, don't wait to be asked, act now, and add reminders to your calendar to complete a calendar audit every 3 months. But for now, enjoy your victory and enjoy looking at your newly optimised calendar. You did it!

Congratulations on completing Executive Assistant Mastery!

Your dedication and commitment, to implementing the 43 steps outlined in this book, have empowered you to become an executive assistant master. 🏆 As an experienced executive assistant myself, I understand the challenges and demands of this pivotal role. To complete the 43 steps, whilst working full time for your executive is a huge accomplishment. Your determination and tenacity have brought you to this moment of achievement, and I whole heartedly congratulate you on completing the 43 steps! 👏

By adopting the productivity hacks, building solid calendar foundations, managing business travel seamlessly, mastering calendar optimisation, grasping the rhythms of business, and commanding recurring meetings, you've not only enhanced your own skills, but have also become a vital asset to your business executive.

I invite you to reflect on the transformation you've made throughout this journey. The commitment you've shown to your professional development is commendable, and the impact on your career is substantial. You are now the indispensable executive assistant that your manager simply can't be without.

Be proud of what you've accomplished, and for taking the time to invest in your own personal development. You've transformed the support you provide to your exec, and have made the biggest impact possible within 90 days.

As you reflect on your achievements, I encourage you to share your feedback on the 43 step process with others. Your insights are invaluable, and can inspire fellow EAs on their own journeys to mastery. Please leave a customer review on Amazon, and share your thoughts via social media.

Once again, congratulations on completing "Executive Assistant Mastery" and for channelling its transformational power. Use that power to your advantage, and when your next performance review approaches, re-visit this book and remind yourself of all the positive changes you've made, and how they contributed to your executive's success. Document those changes, and use them as evidence of your EA mastery in your performance review.

Wishing you continued EA success,

Maria Fuller
Author of "How to be a PA" and "Executive Assistant Mastery"
November 2023

Chat GPT: Friend or Foe?

I started writing this book in December 2022, and at that time I wasn't using Chat GPT. It wasn't even on my radar. However, today in November 2023, I use it every day. It's an amazing free tool that helps me with a host of different things, both for business and for my personal life.

I decided not to give Chat GPT a standalone step, in the 43 step process, because it's a bit like dedicating a step to 'how to use Google' or 'how to use MS 365'. Chat GPT in my opinion - is a tool. A very useful tool, but a tool nonetheless, and it's not going to do your job for you. But it can save you time, if you know when to use it.

I asked my new friend Chat GPT the following question:

"List 10 examples where executive assistants can save time using Chat GPT for business reasons. Please keep the answer concise."

ChatGPT replied: "Certainly, here are ten examples where executive assistants can save time using Chat GPT for business reasons:

1 **Scheduling Assistance:** GPT can help with scheduling meetings, coordinating calendars, and sending calendar invites.
2 **Email Management:** It can assist in drafting, organizing, and responding to emails more efficiently.
3 **Research Support:** GPT can quickly gather information, market insights, and reports.
4 **Meeting Agendas:** It can generate meeting agendas and prepare briefing documents.
5 **Travel Planning:** GPT can assist with booking flights, hotels, and transportation arrangements.
6 **Expense Reports:** It can help compile and organize expense reports.

Made in the USA
Las Vegas, NV
24 January 2024

84864502R00138